THE UK NINJA SPEEDI

COOKBOOK

WITH PICTURES

1500 Days Fast & Tasty Speedi Rapid Recipes with Tips & Tricks and 4-Week Meal Plan to Air Fry, Grill, Bake/Roast, and Sear/Sauté at Ease

Kate Owen

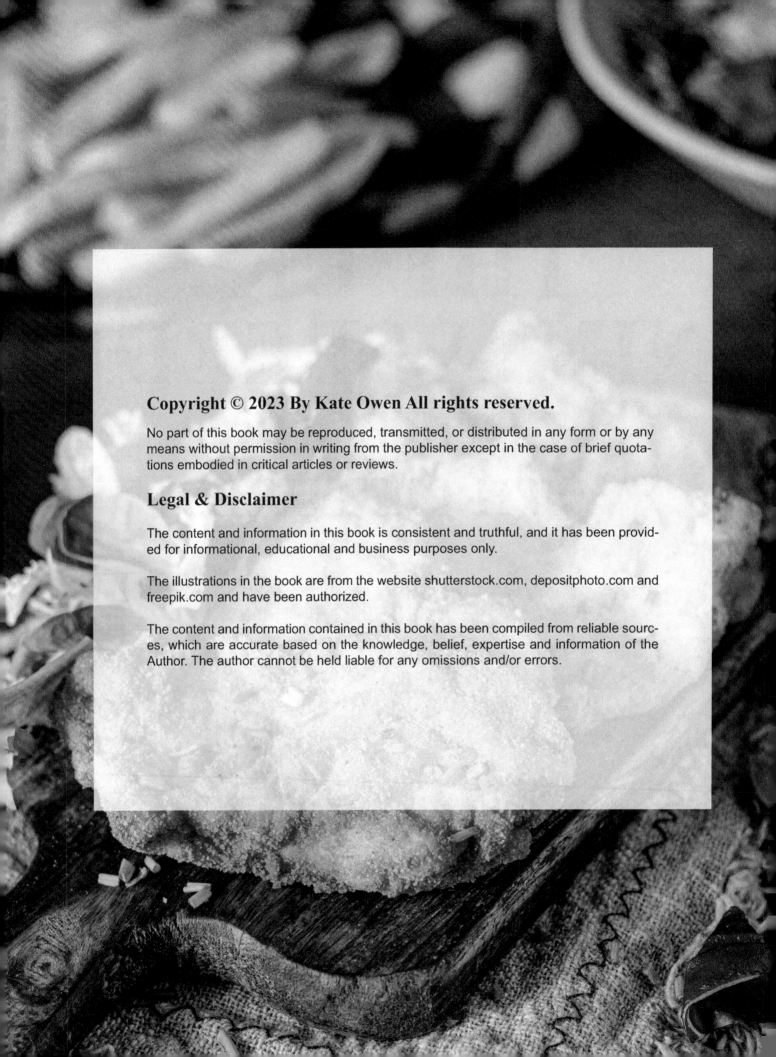

TABLE OF

CONTENT

INTRODUCTION

Welcome to this cookbook for the Ninja Speedi Rapid Cooker & Air Fryer! This versatile kitchen appliance allows you to create a wide range of delicious and healthy meals with ease. Whether you're cooking for your family, entertaining guests, or meal prepping for the week, the Ninja Speedi 10-in-1 Rapid Cooker & Air Fryer is the perfect tool for the job.

With its 10 different functions, including air frying, slow cooking, roasting, baking, and more, this appliance makes it easy to prepare all kinds of meals. From crispy chicken wings to tender pot roasts to fluffy baked potatoes, the Ninja Speedi Rapid Cooker & Air Fryer can do it all.

So, let's get started! Whether you're an experienced cook or a beginner, this recipe is sure to impress. Follow the instructions carefully, and don't forget to read the safety guidelines in your user manual before using your Ninja Speedi Rapid Cooker & Air Fryer.

CHAPTER 1:
BASIC OF THE NINJA SPEEDI RAPID COOKER AND AIR FRYER

The Ninja Speedi Rapid Cooker and Air Fryer is a versatile kitchen appliance that combines the power of superheated steam and air frying to cook food quickly and evenly. It offers multiple cooking functions, including air frying, roasting, baking, grilling, steaming, and sautéing, making it perfect for preparing a wide range of meals. The appliance has a large 5.7-litre capacity, making it ideal for cooking meals for the whole family. It also has preset cooking programmes for popular meals such as roast chicken, chips, and fish, making it easy to cook your favourite dishes.

With its Rapid Cooking System, the Ninja Speedi can cook meals up to 60% faster than traditional cooking methods, which means you can enjoy delicious meals in a fraction of the time. Additionally, the appliance allows you to enjoy your favourite fried foods with up to 75% less fat than traditional frying methods, making it a healthier cooking option. The Ninja Speedi Rapid Cooker and Air Fryer is easy to clean, with a non-stick cooking pot and accessories. Its compact design makes it a great addition to any kitchen without taking up too much counter space.

Overall, the Ninja Speedi Rapid Cooker and Air Fryer is a great addition to any kitchen that can help you save time, eat healthier, and enjoy delicious meals every day.

Benefits of Ninja Speedi Rapid Cooker

The Ninja Speedi Rapid Cooker and Air Fryer boasts the ability to create mouth-watering one-pot meals in just 30 minutes, making it an ideal choice for everyday cooking. Additionally, it offers numerous benefits including:

- **Multiple cooking options**
The Ninja Speedi Rapid Cooker and Air Fryer offers 10 different cooking options, including Speedi Meals, Steam Air Fry, Steam Bake, Steam, Grill, Air Fry, Bake/Roast, Dehydrate, Sear/Sauté, and Slow Cook.

- **Easy to operate**
The touchscreen on the front of the unit makes it easy to select and adjust cooking functions, cooking time, and temperature.

- **Versatile**
The Ninja Speedi Rapid Cooker and Air Fryer can be used as an oven, hob, steamer, air fryer, and more, making it a versatile addition to any kitchen.

- **Healthier cooking**
The air frying function allows you to cook food with little to no oil, making it a healthier alternative to traditional frying.

- **Large capacity**

The unit has a 5.7-litre cooking pot, which is large enough to cook meals for a family or group of friends.

- **Easy to clean**

The cooking pot, crisper tray, and condensation catch can all be cleaned in a dishwasher, making clean up quick and easy.

- **Saves space**

The Ninja Speedi Rapid Cooker and Air Fryer can replace multiple appliances in the kitchen, saving space and reducing clutter.

- **Even cooking**

The Speedi Meals setting allows for simultaneous cooking on two different levels, ensuring even cooking and perfect results.

Cooking Tips and Tricks

When it comes to cooking with the Ninja Speedi, there are many tips and tricks that can help you make the most out of this versatile appliance. The most surprising feature of this appliance is that it can simultaneously air-fry and steam food, allowing you to cook Speedi Meals with grains, vegetables, and meats on two different levels by combining the two cooking options.

In addition to this, the Ninja Speedi offers a variety of cooking settings, including Speedi Meals, Steam Air Fry, Steam Bake, Steam, Grill, Air Fry, Bake/Roast, Dehydrate, Sear/Sauté, and Slow Cook. Depending on the function you choose to use, you can switch between the Air Fry (convection) and Rapid Cooker (steam convection) modes using a lever on the lid.

The Ninja Speedi also has a touchscreen on the front that can be used to operate all 10 features. Here's a breakdown of each cooking function and some tips for using them:

SPEEDI MEALS: This function is perfect for creating quick and delicious meals in under 30 minutes. To get the best results, make sure you use small cuts of meat and chop your vegetables into small pieces.

STEAM AIR FRY: Use this function to create a combination of juicy and crispy results. When using this function, it's important to make sure you don't overcrowd the Cook & Crisp Tray to ensure even cooking.

STEAM BAKE: This function is great for baking fluffy cakes and quick breads. When using this function, make sure you use the correct baking temperature and time.

STEAM: This function gently cooks delicate foods at a high temperature. To get the best results, make sure you use the Cook & Crisp Tray and don't overcook your food.

GRILL: Use high heat from above to caramelise and brown the tops of your food. When using this function, please keep an eye on your food to prevent burning.

AIR FRY: This function gives food crispness and crunch with little to no oil. When using this function, make sure you shake the food regularly to ensure even cooking.

BAKE/ROAST: Use this function like an oven with dry heat for tender meats, baked treats and more. When using this function, make sure you use the correct temperature and cooking time.

DEHYDRATE: Use this function to dehydrate meats, fruits and vegetables for healthy snacks. When using this function, make sure you slice your food evenly and set the correct temperature and time.

SEAR/SAUTÉ: Use this function as a hob for browning meats, sautéing vegetables, simmering sauces and more. When using this function, make sure you use a flat surface and don't overcrowd the cooking area.

SLOW COOK: This function allows you to cook your food at a lower temperature for a longer period of time. When using this function, make sure you use the correct temperature and cooking time for your recipe.

Getting Started

Congratulations on your new appliance! Here's a step-by-step guide to help you get started with your Ninja Speedi.

Unboxing and Setup:

Remove and discard any packaging material and tape from the unit. Some stickers are to be permanently kept on the unit, ONLY remove stickers with 'peel here'. Before using the appliance, wipe the outer surface with a damp cloth and dry thoroughly.

Safety Precautions:

Pay particular attention to operational instructions, warnings and important safeguards to avoid any injury or property damage. Do not operate the appliance if it is damaged or has a damaged cord or plug. If the appliance malfunctions, stops working, or shows signs of damage, stop using it immediately and contact the manufacturer.

Cleaning:

Wash the removable pot, Cook & Crisp tray and condensation collector in warm, soapy water, then rinse and dry thoroughly. Before using the appliance, ensure that all parts are properly cleaned and dried.

Assembly:

To assemble the Ninja Speedi Rapid Cooker and Air Fryer, simply place the removable pot into the appliance base. Place the Cook & Crisp Tray in the top/bottom position. To install the condensation collector, slide it into the slot on the cooker base. Slide it out to remove it for hand-washing after each use.

Disassembly:

To disassemble the Ninja Speedi Rapid Cooker and Air Fryer, first ensure that the appliance has cooled down completely. Open the lid, remove the Cook & Crisp Tray from the pot, and then remove the pot from the appliance base.

Smart Switch:

The Ninja Speedi Rapid Cooker and Air Fryer features the Smart Switch, which allows you to access different cooking functions based on the position of the handle. By keeping the handle pointing upwards, you can unlock the Speedi Meals, Steam Air Fry, Steam Bake, and Steam cooking functions. After that, turning the Smart Switch to the downward position unlocks the Grill, Air Fry, Bake/Roast, Dehydrate, Sear/Sauté, and Slow Cook options.

Control Panel:

The control panel is easy to use and allows you to select various cooking modes and adjust cooking times and temperatures. The panel includes buttons for functions like speedi meals, air fry, bake/roast, steam, slow cook, sear/sauté, and dehydrate. The digital display shows the current cooking mode, cooking time, and temperature.

Troubleshooting:

If you encounter any problems while using your Ninja Speedi, refer to the user manual for troubleshooting tips. Common issues include error messages, loose or missing components, power supply issues, and steaming release problems. If you are unable to resolve the problem, contact the manufacturer for assistance.

In summary, it is crucial to follow the instruction manual carefully when setting up and using the appliance to avoid any mishaps. If you encounter any issues, don't hesitate to contact customer support for help.

Maintenance and Cleaning

The maintenance and cleaning section is important to keep your Ninja Speedi appliance running smoothly. After each cooking session, it is necessary to clean the appliance completely. Firstly, unplug the appliance from the wall socket and make sure it has cooled down completely. Wipe a moist towel over the control panel and cooker base to clean them.

To clean the removable parts such as the cooking pot, Cook & Crisp tray, and condensation collector, use a dishwasher. Before washing, fill the pot with water and let it soak if food residue is stuck to the pot or Cook & Crisp tray. Avoid using scouring pads and if required, use a nylon pad or brush with liquid dish soap or non-abrasive cleaner.

It is recommended to clean the interior of the lid before using the wet cooking functions such as Slow Cook, Sear/ Sauté, and all Rapid Cooker settings. Check the interior of the lid for any food residue or oil buildup on the heating element or fan, and wipe it down with a clean cloth.

For steam cleaning, add 700ml of water to the pot and change the Smart Switch to the Rapid Cooker. Select STEAM and set the time to 30 minutes, and press START/STOP. After the clock hits zero and the appliance has cooled down, use any damp cloth or sponge to clean the interior of the lid. Avoid touching the fan while cleaning the lid's interior. To ensure that all residue has been removed, drain the water from the pot and rinse both the cooking pot and Cook & Crisp tray.

Frequently Asked Questions

This section could address common questions or concerns that readers may have about the Ninja Speedi.

Q: Can I use the Ninja Speedi Rapid Cooker for pressure cooking?

A: No, the Ninja Speedi does not have a pressure cooking function. But it is have 10 functions including speedi meals, steam bake, air fry, bake/roast, slow cook, dehydrate and more.

Q: How do I troubleshoot if my food is not cooking properly?

A: If you find that your food is not cooking properly, it could be due to a number of reasons such as incorrect temperature or time settings, overloading the unit, or not preheating the unit long enough. Refer to the user manual for troubleshooting tips and ensure that you are following the instructions for the specific cooking function you are using.

Q: Can I adapt my own recipes to work with the Ninja Speedi Rapid Cooker?

A: Yes, you can adapt your own recipes to work with the Ninja Speedi Rapid Cooker. However, it is important to note that cooking times and temperatures may need to be adjusted depending on the specific cooking function you are using. Refer to the user manual for guidance on adapting recipes and adjusting cooking settings.

Q: Can I use the Ninja Speedi Rapid Cooker to bake cakes and breads?

A: Yes, the Steam Bake function is specifically designed for baking fluffy cakes and quick breads.

Q: Can I cook frozen food in the Ninja Speedi?

A: Yes, the Air Fry function can be used to cook frozen foods quickly and with crisp results, without the need for thawing.

Conclusion

As we come to the end of this cookbook, we want to express our gratitude to all of our readers for choosing the Ninja Speedi as their go-to cooking partner. We hope that the recipes and tips provided in this cookbook have helped you to unlock the full potential of this versatile appliance and inspire you to explore new culinary horizons.

Remember to experiment with different cooking functions and techniques to achieve the perfect results every time. Don't be afraid to get creative and adapt your favourite recipes to work with the Ninja Speedi's features. Whether you're a seasoned cook or a beginner, this appliance makes cooking quick, easy and enjoyable.

Before we say goodbye, we would like to leave you with a final piece of advice: always read the user manual carefully and follow the safety instructions to ensure that you get the most out of your Ninja Speedi in a safe and responsible manner.

Thank you once again for choosing the Ninja Speedi Rapid Cooker and Air Fryer. We wish you many happy hours of cooking and delicious meals to come!

CHAPTER 2
SPEEDI MEALS

Miso Marinated Steak and Spinach Pasta

SERVES: 2

PREP: 15 minutes
TOTAL COOK TIME: 25 minutes
STEAM: approx. 10 minutes
COOK: 15 minutes

LEVEL 1 (BOTTOM OF POT)
225 g legume based pasta
60 g spinach
750 ml water
LEVEL 2 (TRAY)
cooking spray
340 g flank steak
20 ml sake

15 ml brown miso paste
5 ml honey
2 cloves garlic, pressed
15 ml olive oil
TOPPINGS:
Sesame seeds
Sour cream

1. Place all Level 1 ingredients in the pot and stir to combine.
2. Pull out the legs on the Cook & Crisp tray, then place the tray in the top position in the pot.
3. Put all Level 2 ingredients in a Ziploc bag. Shake to cover the steak well with the seasonings and refrigerate for at least 1 hour.
4. Coat all sides of the steak with cooking spray. Put the steak on top of the tray.
5. Close the lid and flip the SmartSwitch to RAPID COOKER.
6. Select SPEEDI MEALS, set temperature to 190°C, and set time to 15 minutes. Press START/STOP to begin cooking (the unit will steam for approx. 10 minutes, before countdown time begins).
7. When cooking is complete, remove the steak from the tray. Then use silicone-tipped tongs to grab the centre handle and remove the tray from the unit. Transfer the pasta and spinach to a bowl, then top with the steak and desired toppings.

Beef Bratwursts with Quinoa

SERVES: 4

PREP: 10 minutes
TOTAL COOK TIME: 25 minutes
STEAM: approx. 10 minutes
COOK: 15 minutes

LEVEL 1 (BOTTOM OF POT)
375 ml water or stock
200 g quinoa
110 g shredded cheddar cheese
55 g butter, cubed
Ground black pepper, as desired
coarse salt, as desired
LEVEL 2 (TRAY)
4 (85-g) beef bratwursts

1. Place all Level 1 ingredients in the pot and stir to combine.
2. Pull out the legs on the Cook & Crisp tray, then place the tray in the top position in the pot.
3. Place the beef bratwursts on top of the tray.
4. Close the lid and flip the SmartSwitch to RAPID COOKER.
5. Select SPEEDI MEALS, set temperature to 190°C, and set time to 15 minutes. Press START/STOP to begin cooking (the unit will steam for approx. 10 minutes, before countdown time begins).
6. When cooking is complete, remove the beef bratwursts from the tray. Then use silicone-tipped tongs to grab the centre handle and remove the tray from the unit. Transfer the quinoa to a bowl, then top with the beef bratwursts.
7. Serve hot.

Five Spice Pork and Quinoa with Asparagus

SERVES: 4

PREP: 10 minutes

TOTAL COOK TIME: 25 minutes

STEAM: approx. 10 minutes

COOK: 15 minutes

LEVEL 1 (BOTTOM OF POT)
200 g quinoa, rinsed
1 small bunch asparagus, trimmed
375 ml water
15 ml olive oil
Salt and ground black pepper, as required
LEVEL 2 (TRAY)
450 g pork belly
2 tbsps. swerve

30 ml dark soy sauce
15 ml Shaoxing (cooking wine)
2 tsps. garlic, minced
2 tsps. ginger, minced
15 ml hoisin sauce
1 tsp. Chinese Five Spice
TOPPINGS:
Hummus
Sesame seeds

1. Place all Level 1 ingredients in the pot and stir to combine.
2. Pull out the legs on the Cook & Crisp tray, then place the tray in the top position in the pot.
3. Mix all the ingredients in a bowl and place in the Ziplock bag.
4. Seal the bag, shake it well and refrigerate to marinate for about 1 hour.
5. Remove the pork from the bag and arrange on top of the tray.
6. Close the lid and flip the SmartSwitch to RAPID COOKER.
7. Select SPEEDI MEALS, set temperature to 190°C, and set time to 20 minutes. Press START/STOP to begin cooking (the unit will steam for approx. 10 minutes, before countdown time begins).
8. When cooking is complete, remove the pork from the tray. Then use silicone-tipped tongs to grab the centre handle and remove the tray from the unit. Transfer the quinoa and asparagus to a bowl, then top with the pork and desired toppings.

Glazed Pork and Broccoli Rice

SERVES: 4

PREP: 20 minutes

TOTAL COOK TIME: 30 minutes

STEAM: approx. 10 minutes

COOK: 20 minutes

LEVEL 1 (BOTTOM OF POT)
240 g jasmine rice, rinsed
160 g fresh broccoli, cut into 5 cm florets
500 ml water
LEVEL 2 (TRAY)
900 g pork shoulder, cut into 4 cm thick slices
80 ml soy sauce
25 g sugar
15 ml honey

1. Place all Level 1 ingredients in the pot and stir to combine.
2. Pull out the legs on the Cook & Crisp tray, then place the tray in the top position in the pot.
3. Mix all the ingredients in a large bowl and coat the pork well.
4. Cover and refrigerate for about 8 hours.
5. Arrange the pork on top of the tray.
6. Close the lid and flip the SmartSwitch to RAPID COOKER.
7. Select SPEEDI MEALS, set temperature to 190°C, and set time to 20 minutes. Press START/STOP to begin cooking (the unit will steam for approx. 10 minutes, before countdown time begins).
8. When cooking is complete, remove the pork from the tray. Then use silicone-tipped tongs to grab the centre handle and remove the tray from the unit. Transfer the rice and broccoli to a bowl, then top with the pork.
9. Serve hot.

Paprika Chicken Drumsticks with Chickpea Rice

SERVES: 4

PREP: 20 minutes

TOTAL COOK TIME: 35-40 minutes

STEAM: approx. 10-15 minutes

COOK: 25 minutes

LEVEL 1 (BOTTOM OF POT)
120 g tinned chickpeas
1.1 L water
240 g deseeded and minced ripe tomato
Salt and pepper, to taste
300 g rinsed and drained white rice

LEVEL 2 (TRAY)
¼ tsp. dried thyme
1½ tbsps. paprika
Salt and pepper, to taste
½ tsp. onion powder
4 (140-170 g each) chicken drumsticks

1. Place all Level 1 ingredients in the pot and stir to combine.
2. Pull out the legs on the Cook & Crisp tray, then place the tray in the top position in the pot.
3. On a clean work surface, rub the chicken drumsticks generously with the spices. Season with salt and pepper. Place the chicken on top of the tray.
4. Close the lid and flip the SmartSwitch to RAPID COOKER.
5. Select SPEEDI MEALS, set temperature to 210°C, and set time to 25 minutes. Press START/STOP to begin cooking (the unit will steam for approx. 10 to 15 minutes, before countdown time begins).
6. When cooking is complete, remove the chicken from the tray. Then use silicone-tipped tongs to grab the centre handle and remove the tray from the unit. Transfer the Chickpea Rice to a bowl, then top with the chicken. Serve warm.

Chicken with Butternut Squash Porridge

SERVES: 2

PREP: 15 minutes

TOTAL COOK TIME: 23 to 26 minutes

STEAM: approx. 7 to 10 minutes

COOK: 16 minutes

LEVEL 1 (BOTTOM OF POT)
300 g cubed (1-cm pieces) peeled butternut squash
100 g quick-cooking oats
750 ml water
1 tbsp. chia seeds
60 ml unsweetened nondairy milk
1½ tsps. ground ginger
2 tsps. yellow (mellow) miso paste
1 tbsp. sesame seeds, toasted
1 tbsp. chopped scallion, green parts only

LEVEL 2 (TRAY)
2 frozen breaded chicken breasts

1. Add the butternut squash, oats and water (set aside the cheese packets), and broccoli to the pot. Stir to combine well.
2. Pull out the legs on the Cook & Crisp tray, then place the tray in the top position in the pot above the oatmeal.
3. Place the chicken breasts on top of the tray.
4. Close the lid and flip the SmartSwitch to RAPID COOKER. Select SPEEDI MEALS, set temperature to 200°C, and set time to 16 minutes. Press START/STOP to begin cooking (the unit will steam for approx. 7 to 10 minutes, before countdown time begins).
5. Meanwhile, add the chia seeds, milk, ginger and miso paste into a small bowl, whisk them together to combine.
6. When cooking is complete, remove the chicken from the tray. Then use silicone tipped tongs to remove the Cook & Crisp tray. Transfer the oatmeal to a bowl, Mash the cooked butternut squash with a potato masher or heavy spoon. Stir to combine well with the oats. Stir the milk mixture into the oats.
7. Place the sesame seeds and scallion over the porridge bowl. Serve warm with chicken breast.

Coated Prawn and Cherry Tomato Meal

SERVES: 3

PREP: 20 minutes

TOTAL COOK TIME: 22 minutes

STEAM: approx. 10 minutes

COOK: 12 minutes

LEVEL 1 (BOTTOM OF POT)
200 g Arborio rice, rinsed
1 L water
150 g cherry tomatoes
Salt and black pepper, as required
LEVEL 2 (TRAY)
25 g rice flour

450 g prawn, peeled and deveined
30 ml olive oil
5 g caster sugar
Salt and black pepper, as required
TOPPINGS:
Sour cream
Tzatziki

1. Place all Level 1 ingredients in the pot and stir to combine.
2. Pull out the legs on the Cook & Crisp tray, then place the tray in the top position in the pot.
3. Mix rice flour, olive oil, sugar, salt, and black pepper in a bowl.
4. Stir in the prawn and transfer the prawn on top of the tray.
5. Close the lid and flip the SmartSwitch to RAPID COOKER.
6. Select SPEEDI MEALS, set temperature to 175°C, and set time to 12 minutes. Press START/STOP to begin cooking (the unit will steam for approx. 10 minutes, before countdown time begins).
7. When cooking is complete, remove the prawn from the tray. Then use silicone-tipped tongs to grab the centre handle and remove the tray from the unit. Transfer the rice and cherry tomato to a bowl, then top with the prawn and desired toppings.

Scallops with Spinach and Quinoa

SERVES: 2

PREP: 20 minutes

TOTAL COOK TIME: 16 minutes

STEAM: approx. 10 minutes

COOK: 6 minutes

LEVEL 1 (BOTTOM OF POT)
175 g quinoa, rinsed
350 ml water or stock
Salt and ground black pepper, as required
LEVEL 2 (TRAY)
340g frozen spinach, thawed and drained
8 jumbo sea scallops

175 ml double cream
1 tbsp. fresh basil, chopped
Cooking spray
Salt and ground black pepper, as required
15 ml tomato paste
1 tsp. garlic, minced

1. Place all Level 1 ingredients in the pot and stir to combine.
2. Pull out the legs on the Cook & Crisp tray, then place the tray in the top position in the pot. Spray the tray with cooking spray.
3. Season the scallops evenly with salt and black pepper.
4. Mix cream, tomato paste, garlic, basil, salt, and black pepper in a bowl.
5. Place spinach on top of the tray, followed by seasoned scallops and top with the cream mixture.
6. Close the lid and flip the SmartSwitch to RAPID COOKER.
7. Select SPEEDI MEALS, set temperature to 200°C, and set time to 6 minutes. Press START/STOP to begin cooking (the unit will steam for approx. 10 minutes, before countdown time begins).
8. When cooking is complete, remove the scallops and spinach from the tray. Then use silicone-tipped tongs to grab the centre handle and remove the tray from the unit. Transfer the quinoa to a bowl, then top with the scallops and spinach.
9. Serve hot.

Asian Chicken with Courgette Pasta

SERVES: 4

PREP: 20 minutes

TOTAL COOK TIME: 25 minutes

STEAM: approx. 10 minutes

COOK: 15 minutes

LEVEL 1 (BOTTOM OF POT)
15 g butter
1 yellow onion, thinly sliced
Salt and black pepper, to taste
2 garlic cloves, minced
1 courgette, thinly sliced
Pinch of dried basil
875 ml water
30 ml soy sauce
425 g penne pasta

140 g tomato paste
LEVEL 2 (TRAY)
3 minced garlic cloves
680 g boneless chicken breasts
45 ml soy sauce
1 tbsp. ginger slices
TOPPINGS:
Fresh herbs
Salsa
Guacamole

1. Place all Level 1 ingredients in the pot and stir to combine.
2. Pull out the legs on the Cook & Crisp tray, then place the tray in the top position in the pot.
3. Season the chicken breasts with garlic, soy sauce, and ginger slices. Place the chicken breasts on top of the tray.
4. Close the lid and flip the SmartSwitch to RAPID COOKER.
5. Select SPEEDI MEALS, set temperature to 200°C, and set time to 15 minutes. Press START/STOP to begin cooking (the unit will steam for approx. 10 minutes, before countdown time begins).
6. When cooking is complete, remove the chicken breasts from the tray. Then use silicone-tipped tongs to grab the centre handle and remove the tray from the unit. Transfer the Courgette Pasta to a bowl, then top with the chicken breasts and toppings.

Pine Nut Pork and Olive Pasta

SERVES: 4

PREP: 25 minutes

TOTAL COOK TIME: 30-35 minutes

STEAM: approx. 10-15 minutes

COOK: 20 minutes

LEVEL 1 (BOTTOM OF POT)
3 cloves garlic, minced
480 g pasta such as penne or fusilli (short pasta)
1 L pasta sauce (homemade or store-bought)
1 L water
1 tbsp. of capers
80 g Kalamata olives, sliced
¼ tsp. crushed red pepper flakes

LEVEL 1 (BOTTOM OF POT)
3 cloves garlic, minced
480 g pasta such as penne or fusilli (short pasta)
1 L pasta sauce (homemade or store-bought)
1 L water
1 tbsp. of capers
80 g Kalamata olives, sliced
¼ tsp. crushed red pepper flakes

1. Place all Level 1 ingredients in the pot and stir to combine.
2. Pull out the legs on the Cook & Crisp tray, then place the tray in the top position in the pot.
3. In a large bowl, mix the pork tenderloin with the remaining ingredients. Place the pork tenderloin on top of the tray.
4. Close the lid and flip the SmartSwitch to RAPID COOKER.
5. Select SPEEDI MEALS, set temperature to 190°C, and set time to 20 minutes. Press START/STOP to begin cooking (the unit will steam for approx. 10 to 15 minutes, before countdown time begins).
6. When cooking is complete, remove the pork tenderloin from the tray. Then use silicone-tipped tongs to grab the centre handle and remove the tray from the unit. Transfer the pasta mixture to a bowl, then top with the pork tenderloin.
7. Serve hot.

Bacon Wrapped Filet Mignon with Bean Rice

SERVES: 2

PREP: 25 minutes TOTAL COOK TIME: 25 minutes STEAM: approx. 10 minutes COOK: 15 minutes	**LEVEL 1 (BOTTOM OF POT)** 200 g white rice, rinsed 240 g tinned black beans, drained 500 ml water or stock **LEVEL 2 (TRAY)** 2 rashers of bacon 2 (170 g) filet mignon steaks Salt and black pepper, to taste 5 ml avocado oil **TOPPINGS:** Fresh herbs Salsa Sour Cream

1. Place all Level 1 ingredients in the pot and stir to combine.
2. Pull out the legs on the Cook & Crisp tray, then place the tray in the top position in the pot.
3. Wrap each mignon steak with 1 rasher of bacon and secure with a toothpick.
4. Season the steak generously with salt and black pepper and coat with avocado oil.
5. Arrange the steaks on top of the tray.
6. Close the lid and flip the SmartSwitch to RAPID COOKER.
7. Select SPEEDI MEALS, set temperature to 190°C, and set time to 15 minutes. Press START/STOP to begin cooking (the unit will steam for approx. 10 minutes, before countdown time begins).
8. When cooking is complete, remove the steaks from the tray and cut into desired size slices. Then use silicone-tipped tongs to grab the centre handle and remove the tray from the unit. Transfer the rice and beans to a bowl, then top with the steaks and toppings.

Spiced Lamb Steaks and Snap Pea Rice

SERVES: 3

PREP: 15 minutes TOTAL COOK TIME: 25 minutes STEAM: approx. 10 minutes COOK: 15 minutes	**LEVEL 1 (BOTTOM OF POT)** 200 g easy-cooked brown rice, rinsed 200 g sugar snap peas 500 ml water Salt, to taste **LEVEL 2 (TRAY)** ½ onion, roughly chopped 680 g boneless lamb sirloin steaks 5 garlic cloves, peeled 1 tbsp. fresh ginger, peeled 1 tsp. garam masala 1 tsp. ground fennel ½ tsp. ground cumin ½ tsp. ground cinnamon ½ tsp. cayenne pepper Salt and black pepper, to taste **TOPPINGS:** Mint sauce Greek yogurt

1. Put the onion, garlic, ginger, and spices in a blender and pulse until smooth.
2. Coat the lamb steaks with this mixture on both sides and refrigerate to marinate for about 24 hours.
3. Place all Level 1 ingredients in the pot and stir to combine.
4. Pull out the legs on the Cook & Crisp tray, then place the tray in the top position in the pot.
5. Arrange the lamb steaks on top of the tray.
6. Close the lid and flip the SmartSwitch to RAPID COOKER.
7. Select SPEEDI MEALS, set temperature to 180°C, and set time to 15 minutes. Press START/STOP to begin cooking (the unit will steam for approx. 10 minutes, before countdown time begins).
8. When cooking is complete, remove the lamb steaks from the tray. Then use silicone-tipped tongs to grab the centre handle and remove the tray from the unit. Transfer the brown rice and snap peas to a bowl, then top with the lamb steaks and desired toppings.

Pesto Coated Rack of Lamb and Farfalle

SERVES: 4

PREP: 15 minutes
TOTAL COOK TIME: 30 minutes
STEAM: approx. 10 minutes
COOK: 20 minutes

LEVEL 1 (BOTTOM OF POT)
225 g Farfalle pasta
120 ml tomato sauce
30 g fresh spinach
500 ml water
LEVEL 2 (TRAY)
½ bunch fresh mint
1 (680 g) rack of lamb

1 garlic clove
60 ml extra-virgin olive oil
7 ml honey
Salt and black pepper, to taste
TOPPINGS:
Mint sauce
Sour cream

1. Place all Level 1 ingredients in the pot and stir to combine.
2. Pull out the legs on the Cook & Crisp tray, then place the tray in the top position in the pot.
3. Put the mint, garlic, oil, honey, salt, and black pepper in a blender and pulse until smooth to make pesto.
4. Coat the rack of lamb with this pesto on both sides and arrange on top of the tray.
5. Close the lid and flip the SmartSwitch to RAPID COOKER.
6. Select SPEEDI MEALS, set temperature to 180°C, and set time to 20 minutes. Press START/STOP to begin cooking (the unit will steam for approx. 10 minutes, before countdown time begins).
7. When cooking is complete, remove the rack from the tray. Cut the rack into individual chops. Then use silicone-tipped tongs to grab the centre handle and remove the tray from the unit. Transfer the pasta and spinach to a bowl, then top with the chops and desired toppings.

Garlic-Lemon Tilapia with Mushroom Rice

SERVES: 4

PREP: 15 minutes
TOTAL COOK TIME: 22 minutes
STEAM: approx. 10 minutes
COOK: 12 minutes

LEVEL 1 (BOTTOM OF POT)
180 g brown rice, rinsed
150 g frozen mushrooms
375 ml water
LEVEL 2 (TRAY)
15 ml lemon juice
15 ml olive oil

1 tsp. minced garlic
½ tsp. chilli powder
4 (170-g each) tilapia fillets
TOPPINGS:
Horseradish
Hummus

1. Place all Level 1 ingredients in the pot and stir to combine.
2. Pull out the legs on the Cook & Crisp tray, then place the tray in the top position in the pot.
3. In a large, shallow bowl, mix together the lemon juice, olive oil, garlic, and chilli powder to make a marinade. Place the tilapia fillets in the bowl and coat evenly. Place the fillets on top of the tray.
4. Close the lid and flip the SmartSwitch to RAPID COOKER.
5. Select SPEEDI MEALS, set temperature to 180°C, and set time to 12 minutes. Press START/STOP to begin cooking (the unit will steam for approx. 10 minutes, before countdown time begins).
6. When cooking is complete, remove the tilapia fillets from the tray. Then use silicone-tipped tongs to grab the centre handle and remove the tray from the unit. Transfer the rice and mushroom to a bowl, then top with the tilapia fillets and desired toppings.

Salmon and Bok Choy Meal

SERVES: 4

PREP: 10 minutes
TOTAL COOK TIME: 24-29 minutes
STEAM: approx. 10-15 minutes
COOK: 14 minutes

LEVEL 1 (BOTTOM OF POT)
400 g wild rice, soaked in water overnight and drained
1 L water
75 g sultanas
200 g Bok choy, sliced
55 g salted butter
1 tsp. salt

LEVEL 2 (TRAY)
30 g unsalted butter
4 (2.5 cm thick) salmon fillets
½ tsp. cayenne pepper
Sea salt and freshly ground pepper, to taste
3 cloves garlic, minced
1 tsp. grated lemon zest
½ tsp. dried dill weed

1. Place all Level 1 ingredients in the pot and stir to combine.
2. Pull out the legs on the Cook & Crisp tray, then place the tray in the top position in the pot.
3. Brush the salmon with the melted butter and season with the cayenne pepper, salt, and black pepper on all sides. Place the salmon on top of the tray. Top with the remaining ingredients.
4. Close the lid and flip the SmartSwitch to RAPID COOKER.
5. Select SPEEDI MEALS, set temperature to 180°C, and set time to 14 minutes. Press START/STOP to begin cooking (the unit will steam for approx. 10 to 15 minutes, before countdown time begins).
6. When cooking is complete, remove the salmon from the tray. Then use silicone-tipped tongs to grab the centre handle and remove the tray from the unit. Transfer the rice and Bok choy to a bowl, then top with the salmon.

CHAPTER 3
STEAM AIR FRY

Cheesy Potato Patties

SERVES: 8

PREP: 5 minutes

TOTAL COOK TIME: 12 minutes

STEAM: approx. 4 minutes

COOK: 8 minutes

125 ml water, for steaming
907 g white potatoes
120 ml finely chopped scallions
½ tsp. freshly ground black pepper, or more to taste
1 tbsp. fine sea salt

½ tsp. hot paprika
226 g shredded Colby cheese
60 ml rapeseed oil
120 g crushed crackers

1. Pour 125 ml water into the pot. Push in the legs on the Cook & Crisp tray, then place the tray in the bottom position in the pot.
2. Boil the potatoes until soft. Dry them off and peel them before mashing thoroughly, leaving no lumps.
3. Combine the mashed potatoes with scallions, pepper, salt, paprika, and cheese.
4. Mold the mixture into balls with your hands and press with your palm to flatten them into patties.
5. In a shallow dish, combine the rapeseed oil and crushed crackers. Coat the patties in the crumb mixture. Place the patties on the tray.
6. Close the lid and flip the SmartSwitch to RAPID COOKER. Select STEAM AIR FRY, set temperature to 190°C, and set time to 8 minutes. Press START/STOP to begin cooking (the unit will steam for approx. 4 minutes, before countdown time begins).
7. When cooking is complete, use tongs to remove the patties from the tray and serve hot.

Amazing Salmon Fillets

SERVES: 2

PREP: 5 minutes

TOTAL COOK TIME: 12 minutes

STEAM: approx. 4 minutes

COOK: 8 minutes

65 ml water, for steaming
2 (200g) (2-cm thick) salmon fillets
1 tbsp. Italian seasoning
1 tbsp. fresh lemon juice

1. Pour 65 ml water into the pot. Pull out the legs on the Cook & Crisp tray, then place the tray in the top position in the pot.
2. Rub the salmon evenly with Italian seasoning and transfer on the tray, skin-side up.
3. Close the lid and flip the SmartSwitch to RAPID COOKER. Select STEAM AIR FRY, set temperature to 220°C, and set time to 8 minutes. Press START/STOP to begin cooking (the unit will steam for approx. 4 minutes, before countdown time begins).
4. With 4 minutes remaining, open the lid and flip the salmon with tongs. Close the lid to continue cooking.
5. When cooking is complete, use tongs to remove the salmon from the tray. Squeeze lemon juice on it to serve.

Sweet and Sour Glazed Cod

SERVES: 2

PREP: 20 minutes
TOTAL COOK TIME: 14 minutes
STEAM: approx. 4 minutes
COOK: 10 minutes

125 ml water, for steaming
4 (100 g each) cod fillets
5 ml water
80 ml soy sauce
80 ml honey
15 ml rice wine vinegar

1. Mix the soy sauce, honey, vinegar and 5 ml water in a small bowl. Reserve about half of the mixture in another bowl. Stir the cod fillets in the remaining mixture until well coated. Cover and refrigerate to marinate for about 3 hours.
2. Pour 125 ml water into the pot. Pull out the legs on the Cook & Crisp tray, then place the tray in the top position in the pot.
3. Arrange the cod fillets on the tray.
4. Close the lid and flip the SmartSwitch to RAPID COOKER. Select STEAM AIR FRY, set temperature to 220°C, and set time to 10 minutes. Press START/STOP to begin cooking (the unit will steam for approx. 4 minutes, before countdown time begins).
5. With 5 minutes remaining, open the lid and flip the cod with tongs. Close the lid to continue cooking.
6. When cooking is complete, use tongs to remove the cod from the tray.
7. Coat with the reserved marinade and serve hot.

Chicken Manchurian

SERVES: 2

PREP: 10 minutes
TOTAL COOK TIME: 19 minutes
STEAM: approx. 4 minutes
COOK: 15 minutes

125 ml water, for steaming
450 g boneless, skinless chicken breasts, cut into 2.5 cm pieces
60 ml ketchup
1 tbsp. tomato-based chili sauce, such as Heinz
15 ml soy sauce
15 ml rice vinegar
10 ml vegetable oil
1 tsp. hot sauce, such as Tabasco
½ tsp. garlic powder
¼ tsp. cayenne pepper
2 scallions, thinly sliced
Cooked white rice, for serving

1. Pour 125 ml water into the pot. Pull out the legs on the Cook & Crisp tray, then place the tray in the top position in the pot.
2. In a bowl, combine the chicken, ketchup, chili sauce, soy sauce, vinegar, oil, hot sauce, garlic powder, cayenne, and three-quarters of the scallions and toss until evenly coated.
3. Scrape the chicken and sauce into a metal cake pan and place the pan on the tray.
4. Close the lid and flip the SmartSwitch to RAPID COOKER. Select STEAM AIR FRY, set temperature to 190°C, and set time to 15 minutes. Press START/STOP to begin cooking (the unit will steam for approx. 4 minutes, before countdown time begins).
5. With 7 minutes remaining, open the lid and toss the chicken with tongs. Close the lid to continue cooking.
6. When cooking is complete, use tongs to remove the pan from the tray. Spoon the chicken and sauce over rice and top with the remaining scallions. Serve immediately.

Homemade Pulled Pork

PREP: 5 minutes
TOTAL COOK TIME: 29 minutes
STEAM: approx. 4 minutes
COOK: 25 minutes

250 ml water, for steaming
450 g pork tenderloin
80 ml double cream
2 tbsps. barbecue dry rub
5 g butter

1. Pour 250 ml water into the pot. Pull out the legs on the Cook & Crisp tray, then place the tray in the top position in the pot.
2. Massage the dry rub into the tenderloin, coating it evenly.
3. Close the lid and flip the SmartSwitch to RAPID COOKER. Select STEAM AIR FRY, set temperature to 190°C, and set time to 25 minutes. Press START/STOP to begin cooking (the unit will steam for approx. 4 minutes, before countdown time begins).
4. With 5 minutes remaining, open the lid and shred the pork with two forks. Add the double cream and butter into the tray along with the shredded pork and stir well. Close the lid to continue cooking.
5. When cooking is complete, let cool, then serve.

Coconut Crusted Prawn

PREP: 15 minutes
TOTAL COOK TIME: 24 minutes
STEAM: approx. 8 minutes
COOK: 16 minutes

125 ml water, for steaming
225 ml coconut milk
50 g sweetened coconut, shredded
50 g panko breadcrumbs
450 g large prawn, peeled and deveined
Salt and black pepper, to taste

1. Pour 125 ml water into the pot. Push in the legs on the Cook & Crisp tray, then place the tray in the bottom position in the pot.
2. Place the coconut milk in a shallow bowl.
3. Mix coconut, breadcrumbs, salt, and black pepper in another bowl.
4. Dip each prawn into coconut milk and finally, dredge in the coconut mixture.
5. Arrange half of the prawns on the tray.
6. Close the lid and flip the SmartSwitch to RAPID COOKER. Select STEAM AIR FRY, set temperature to 220°C, and set time to 8 minutes. Press START/STOP to begin cooking (the unit will steam for approx. 4 minutes, before countdown time begins).
7. Dish out the prawns onto serving plates.
8. Repeat with the remaining prawns to serve.

Spicy Chicken Bites

PREP: 10 minutes

TOTAL COOK TIME: 19 minutes

STEAM: approx. 4 minutes

COOK: 15 minutes

125 ml water, for steaming
225 g boneless and skinless chicken thighs, cut into 30 pieces
¼ tsp. coarse salt
30 ml hot sauce

1. Pour 125 ml water into the pot. Pull out the legs on the Cook & Crisp tray, then place the tray in the top position in the pot.
2. Season the chicken bites with the coarse salt, then place on the tray.
3. Close the lid and flip the SmartSwitch to RAPID COOKER. Select STEAM AIR FRY, set temperature to 190°C, and set time to 15 minutes. Press START/STOP to begin cooking (the unit will steam for approx. 4 minutes, before countdown time begins).
4. With 8 minutes remaining, open the lid and toss the chicken bites with tongs. Close the lid to continue cooking.
5. While the chicken bites cook, pour the hot sauce into a large bowl.
6. When cooking is complete, use tongs to remove the bites from the tray and add to the sauce bowl, tossing to coat. Serve warm.

Rosemary Duck Breasts

PREP: 15 minutes

TOTAL COOK TIME: 29 minutes

STEAM: approx. 4 minutes

COOK: 25 minutes

125 ml water, for steaming
1 tsp. fresh rosemary, chopped
1 tsp. fresh thyme, chopped
900 g duck breasts
120 ml olive oil
1 tsp. fresh lemon zest, grated finely
¼ tsp. sugar
¼ tsp. red pepper flakes, crushed
Salt and black pepper, to taste

1. Mix all the ingredients in a large bowl except duck breasts.
2. Stir in the duck breasts and refrigerate to marinate well for about 24 hours.
3. Pour 125 ml water into the pot. Pull out the legs on the Cook & Crisp tray, then place the tray in the top position in the pot.
4. Transfer the duck breasts on the tray.
5. Close the lid and flip the SmartSwitch to RAPID COOKER. Select STEAM AIR FRY, set temperature to 200°C, and set time to 25 minutes. Press START/STOP to begin cooking (the unit will steam for approx. 4 minutes, before countdown time begins).
6. With 10 minutes remaining, open the lid and flip the duck breasts with tongs. Close the lid to continue cooking.
7. When cooking is complete, use tongs to remove the duck breasts from the tray and serve hot.

Ranch Dipped Fillets

SERVES: 2

PREP: 5 minutes
TOTAL COOK TIME: 13 minutes
STEAM: approx. 4 minutes
COOK: 9 minutes

125 ml water, for steaming
25 g panko breadcrumbs
1 egg beaten
2 tilapia fillets
½ packet ranch dressing mix powder
18 ml vegetable oil
For Garnish:
Herbs and chilies

1. Pour 125 ml water into the pot. Pull out the legs on the Cook & Crisp tray, then place the tray in the top position in the pot.
2. Mix ranch dressing with panko breadcrumbs in a bowl.
3. Whisk eggs in a shallow bowl and dip the fish fillet in the eggs.
4. Dredge in the breadcrumbs and transfer on the tray.
5. Close the lid and flip the SmartSwitch to RAPID COOKER. Select STEAM AIR FRY, set temperature to 220°C, and set time to 9 minutes. Press START/STOP to begin cooking (the unit will steam for approx. 4 minutes, before countdown time begins).
6. With 4 minutes remaining, open the lid and flip the fillets with tongs. Close the lid to continue cooking.
7. When cooking is complete, transfer the fillets to two serving bowls. Garnish with chilies and herbs to serve.

Pork Neck and Tomato Salad

SERVES: 2

PREP: 20 minutes
TOTAL COOK TIME: 22 minutes
STEAM: approx. 4 minutes
COOK: 8 minutes

125 ml water, for steaming
225 g pork neck
1 ripe tomato, thickly sliced
1 red onion, sliced
1 scallion, chopped
1 bunch fresh basil leaves
15 ml soy sauce
15 ml fish sauce
7 ml oyster sauce

1. Mix all the sauces in a bowl and coat the pork neck in it. Refrigerate for about 3 hours.
2. Pour 125 ml water into the pot. Push in the legs on the Cook & Crisp tray, then place the tray in the bottom position in the pot.
3. Transfer the pork to the tray.
4. Close the lid and flip the SmartSwitch to RAPID COOKER. Select STEAM AIR FRY, set temperature to 190°C, and set time to 18 minutes. Press START/STOP to begin cooking (the unit will steam for approx. 4 minutes, before countdown time begins).
5. With 8 minutes remaining, open the lid and flip the pork with tongs. Close the lid to continue cooking.
6. When cooking is complete, use tongs to remove the pork from the tray. Cut into desired size slices and keep aside.
7. Mix rest of the ingredients in a bowl and top with the pork slices to serve.

Chicken and Pepper Meatballs

PREP: 15 minutes

TOTAL COOK TIME: 20-22 minutes

STEAM: approx. 4 minutes

COOK: 16-18 minutes

250 ml water, for steaming
10 ml olive oil
40 g minced onion
30 g minced red bell pepper
2 vanilla wafers, crushed
1 egg white
½ tsp. dried thyme
225 g chicken breast, minced

1. Pour 125 ml water into the pot. Push in the legs on the Cook & Crisp tray, then place the tray in the bottom position in the pot.
2. In a skillet over medium heat, add the olive oil, onion, and red bell pepper. Sauté for 3 to 5 minutes, until the vegetables are tender.
3. In a medium bowl, mix the cooked vegetables, crushed wafers, egg white, and thyme until well combined.
4. Mix in the chicken, gently but thoroughly, until everything is combined. Form the mixture into 16 meatballs. Place the meatballs on the tray.
5. Close the lid and flip the SmartSwitch to RAPID COOKER. Select STEAM AIR FRY, set temperature to 180°C, and set time to 13 minutes. Press START/STOP to begin cooking (the unit will steam for approx. 4 minutes, before countdown time begins).
6. With 6 minutes remaining, open the lid and flip the side with tongs. Close the lid to continue cooking.
7. Serve immediately.

Turmeric Chicken Thighs

PREP: 10 minutes

TOTAL COOK TIME: 19 minutes

STEAM: approx. 4 minutes

COOK: 15 minutes

125 ml water, for steaming
60 ml julienned peeled fresh ginger
30 ml vegetable oil
15 ml honey
15 ml soy sauce
15 ml ketchup
1 tsp. garam masala

1 tsp. ground turmeric
¼ tsp. coarse salt
½ tsp. cayenne pepper
Vegetable oil spray
450 g boneless, skinless chicken thighs, cut crosswise into thirds
15 g chopped fresh coriander, for garnish

1. In a small bowl, combine the ginger, oil, honey, soy sauce, ketchup, garam masala, turmeric, salt, and cayenne. Whisk until well combined.
2. Place the chicken in a resealable plastic bag and pour the marinade over. Seal the bag and massage to cover all of the chicken with the marinade. Marinate at room temperature for 30 minutes or in the refrigerator for up to 24 hours.
3. Pour 125 ml water into the pot. Pull out the legs on the Cook & Crisp tray, then place the tray in the top position in the pot. Spray the tray with vegetable oil spray
4. Add the chicken and as much of the marinade and julienned ginger as possible to the tray.
5. Close the lid and flip the SmartSwitch to RAPID COOKER. Select STEAM AIR FRY, set temperature to 190°C, and set time to 15 minutes. Press START/STOP to begin cooking (the unit will steam for approx. 4 minutes, before countdown time begins).
6. With 7 minutes remaining, open the lid and toss the chicken with tongs. Close the lid to continue cooking.
7. When cooking is complete, use tongs to remove the chicken from the tray. Serve garnished with coriander.

Italian Lamb Chops with Avocado Mayo

SERVES: 2

PREP: 5 minutes
TOTAL COOK TIME: 24 minutes
STEAM: approx. 4 minutes
COOK: 20 minutes

125 ml water, for steaming
2 lamp chops
2 avocados
120 ml mayonnaise
15 ml lemon juice
2 tsps. Italian herbs

1. Pour 125 ml water into the pot. Push in the legs on the Cook & Crisp tray, then place the tray in the bottom position in the pot.
2. Sprinkle the lamb chops with the Italian herbs, then keep aside for 5 minutes.
3. Close the lid and flip the SmartSwitch to RAPID COOKER. Select STEAM AIR FRY, set temperature to 190°C, and set time to 20 minutes. Press START/STOP to begin cooking (the unit will steam for approx. 4 minutes, before countdown time begins).
4. Meanwhile, halve the avocados and open to remove the pits. Scoop the flesh into a blender. Add the mayonnaise and lemon juice and pulse until a smooth consistency is achieved.
5. Carefully transfer the chops to a plate and serve hot with the avocado mayo.

Bacon Filled Poppers

SERVES: 4

PREP: 5 minutes
TOTAL COOK TIME: 22 minutes
STEAM: approx. 4 minutes
COOK: 18 minutes

125 ml water, for steaming
4 rashers of crispy cooked bacon
45 g butter
60 g jalapeno peppers, diced
70 g almond flour
30 g Cheddar cheese, white, shredded
1 pinch cayenne pepper
1 tbsp. bacon fat
1 tsp. coarse salt
Black pepper, ground, to taste

1. Pour 125 ml water into the pot. Push in the legs on the Cook & Crisp tray, then place the tray in the bottom position in the pot.
2. Mix together butter with salt and water on medium heat in a skillet.
3. Whisk in the flour and sauté for about 3 minutes.
4. Dish out in a bowl and mix with the remaining ingredients to form a dough.
5. Wrap plastic wrap around the dough and refrigerate for about half an hour.
6. Make small popper balls out of this dough and arrange on the tray.
7. Close the lid and flip the SmartSwitch to RAPID COOKER. Select STEAM AIR FRY, set temperature to 200°C, and set time to 15 minutes. Press START/STOP to begin cooking (the unit will steam for approx. 4 minutes, before countdown time begins).
8. With 7 minutes remaining, open the lid and flip the balls with tongs. Close the lid to continue cooking.
9. When cooking is complete, dish out to serve warm.

Cheesy Chicken Stuffed Mushrooms

MAKES: 12 MUSHROOMS

PREP: 10 minutes
TOTAL COOK TIME: 19 minutes
STEAM: approx. 4 minutes
COOK: 15 minutes

125 ml water, for steaming
12 large fresh mushrooms, stems removed
225 g chicken meat, cubed
225 g imitation crabmeat, flaked
450 g butter
Garlic powder, to taste
2 cloves garlic, peeled and minced
Salt and black pepper, to taste
225 g cream cheese, softened
Crushed red pepper, to taste

1. Pour 125 ml water into the pot. Push in the legs on the Cook & Crisp tray, then place the tray in the bottom position in the pot.
2. Heat butter on medium heat in a nonstick skillet and add chicken.
3. Sauté for about 5 minutes and stir in the remaining ingredients except mushrooms.
4. Stuff this filling mixture in the mushroom caps on the tray.
5. Close the lid and flip the SmartSwitch to RAPID COOKER. Select STEAM AIR FRY, set temperature to 190°C, and set time to 10 minutes. Press START/STOP to begin cooking (the unit will steam for approx. 4 minutes, before countdown time begins).
6. When cooking is complete, dish out to serve warm.

CHAPTER 4
STEAM BAKE

Trout Frittata

PREP: 15 minutes

TOTAL COOK TIME: 35 minutes

STEAM: approx. 20 minutes

COOK: 15 minutes

250 ml water, for steaming
cooking spray
1 onion, sliced
6 eggs
2 hot-smoked trout fillets, chopped
25 g fresh dill, chopped
1 tomato, chopped
30 ml olive oil
½ tbsp. horseradish sauce
2 tbsps. crème fraiche

1. Pour 250 ml water into the pot. Push in the legs on the Cook & Crisp tray, then place the tray in the bottom position in the pot. Spray Multi-Purpose Tin or 20cm cake tin with cooking spray.
2. Whisk together eggs with horseradish sauce and crème fraiche in a bowl.
3. Heat olive oil in a pan and add onions.
4. Sauté for about 3 minutes and transfer into the baking pan.
5. Stir in the whisked eggs, trout, tomato and dill.
6. Arrange the tin on the tray.
7. Close the lid and flip the SmartSwitch to RAPID COOKER. Select STEAM BAKE, set temperature to 180°C, and set time to 12 minutes. Press START/STOP to begin cooking (the unit will steam for approx. 20 minutes, before countdown time begins).
8. Dish out and serve hot.

Beef and Mushroom Meatloaf

PREP: 15 minutes

TOTAL COOK TIME: 38 minutes

STEAM: approx. 20 minutes

COOK: 18 minutes

250 ml water, for steaming
cooking spray
450 g lean beef, minced
1 small onion, finely chopped
15 g dry breadcrumbs
1 egg, lightly beaten
2 mushrooms, thickly sliced
Salt and ground black pepper, as required
15 ml olive oil

1. Pour 250 ml water into the pot. Push in the legs on the Cook & Crisp tray, then place the tray in the bottom position in the pot. Spray Multi-Purpose Tin or 20cm cake tin with cooking spray.
2. Mix the beef, onion, olive oil, breadcrumbs, egg, salt, and black pepper in a bowl until well combined.
3. Shape the mixture into loaves and top with mushroom slices.
4. Arrange the loaves in the prepared tin, then place the tin on the tray.
5. Close the lid and flip the SmartSwitch to RAPID COOKER. Select STEAM BAKE, set temperature to 180°C, and set time to 18 minutes. Press START/STOP to begin cooking (the unit will steam for approx. 20 minutes, before countdown time begins).
6. Cut into desired size wedges and serve warm.

Healthy Egg Veggie Frittata

SERVES: 2

PREP: 10 minutes

TOTAL COOK TIME: 35 minutes

STEAM: approx. 20 minutes

COOK: 15 minutes

250 ml water, for steaming
4 eggs
120 ml milk
2 spring onions, chopped
25 g baby Bella mushrooms, chopped
25 g spinach, chopped
15 g butter
½ tsp. salt
½ tsp. black pepper
Dash of hot sauce

1. Pour 250 ml water into the pot. Push in the legs on the Cook & Crisp tray, then place the tray in the bottom position in the pot. Grease a 15x8 cm square pan with butter.
2. Whisk eggs with milk in a large bowl and stir in spring onions, mushrooms and spinach.
3. Sprinkle with salt, black pepper and hot sauce and pour this mixture into the prepared pan. Then place the pan on the tray.
4. Close the lid and flip the SmartSwitch to RAPID COOKER. Select STEAM BAKE, set temperature to 180°C, and set time to 15 minutes. Press START/STOP to begin cooking (the unit will steam for approx. 20 minutes, before countdown time begins).
5. Dish out in a platter and serve warm.

Banana and Walnut Cake

SERVES: 6

PREP: 10 minutes

TOTAL COOK TIME: 45 minutes

STEAM: approx. 20 minutes

COOK: 25 minutes

500 ml water, for steaming
cooking spray
450 g bananas, mashed
225 g plain flour
170 g caster sugar
100 g walnuts, chopped
70 g butter, melted
2 eggs, lightly beaten
¼ tsp. bicarbonate of soda

1. Pour 500 ml water into the pot. Push in the legs on the Cook & Crisp tray, then place the tray in the bottom position in the pot. Spray Multi-Purpose Tin or 20cm cake tin with cooking spray.
2. In a bowl, combine the sugar, butter, egg, flour, and bicarbonate of soda with a whisk. Stir in the bananas and walnuts.
3. Transfer the mixture to the greased tin. Put the tin on the tray.
4. Close the lid and flip the SmartSwitch to RAPID COOKER. Select STEAM BAKE, set temperature to 180°C, and set time to 25 minutes. Press START/STOP to begin cooking (the unit will steam for approx. 20 minutes, before countdown time begins).
5. With 15 minutes remaining, reduce the temperature to 160°C. Continue cooking until the cake is golden down.
6. Serve hot.

Fudgy Chocolaty Squares

SERVES: 4

PREP: 15 minutes
TOTAL COOK TIME: 40 minutes
STEAM: approx. 20 minutes
COOK: 20 minutes

250 ml water, for steaming
cooking spray
55 g cold butter
86 g self-rising flour
7 ml milk
55 g chocolate, chopped
35 g brown sugar
30 ml honey

1. Pour 250 ml water into the pot. Push in the legs on the Cook & Crisp tray, then place the tray in the bottom position in the pot. Spray a tin with cooking spray.
2. Mix butter, brown sugar, flour and honey and beat till smooth.
3. Stir in the chocolate and milk and pour the mixture into a tin, then place the tin on the tray.
4. Close the lid and flip the SmartSwitch to RAPID COOKER. Select STEAM BAKE, set temperature to 160°C, and set time to 20 minutes. Press START/STOP to begin cooking (the unit will steam for approx. 20 minutes, before countdown time begins).
5. Dish out and cut into desired squares to serve.

Heavenly Tasty Lava Cake

SERVES: 6

PREP: 10 minutes
TOTAL COOK TIME: 25 minutes
STEAM: approx. 20 minutes
COOK: 5 minutes

500 ml water, for steaming
cooking spray
150 g unsalted butter
2 eggs
90 g plain flour
175 g chocolate chips, melted
40 g fresh raspberries
75 g caster sugar
Salt, to taste

1. Pour 500 ml water into the pot. Push in the legs on the Cook & Crisp tray, then place the tray in the bottom position in the pot. Spray 6 ramekins with cooking spray.
2. Mix sugar, butter, eggs, chocolate mixture, flour and salt in a bowl until well combined.
3. Fold in the melted chocolate chips and divide this mixture into the prepared ramekins. Transfer the ramekins on the tray.
4. Close the lid and flip the SmartSwitch to RAPID COOKER. Select STEAM BAKE, set temperature to 150°C, and set time to 5 minutes. Press START/STOP to begin cooking (the unit will steam for approx. 20 minutes, before countdown time begins).
5. Garnish with raspberries and serve immediately.

Frosting Cupcakes

SERVES: 12

PREP: 15 minutes

TOTAL COOK TIME: 32 minutes

STEAM: approx. 20 minutes

COOK: 12 minutes

250 ml water, for steaming
cooking spray
For the Cupcakes:
250 g refined flour
170 g peanut butter
3 eggs
90 g icing sugar
2 tsps. beetroot powder

1 tsp. cocoa powder
For the Frosting:
225 g butter
225 g cream cheese
90 g icing sugar
60 ml strawberry sauce
1 tsp. vanilla essence

1. Pour 250 ml water into the pot. Push in the legs on the Cook & Crisp tray, then place the tray in the bottom position in the pot. Spray 12 silicon cups with cooking spray.
2. Mix all the Cupcakes ingredients in a large bowl until well combined.
3. Transfer the mixture into silicon cups and place on the tray.
4. Close the lid and flip the SmartSwitch to RAPID COOKER. Select STEAM BAKE, set temperature to 180°C, and set time to 12 minutes. Press START/STOP to begin cooking (the unit will steam for approx. 20 minutes, before countdown time begins).
5. Mix all the Frosting ingredients in a large bowl until well combined.
6. Top each cupcake evenly with frosting and serve.

Vanilla Blueberry Cake

SERVES: 6

PREP: 10 minutes

TOTAL COOK TIME: 40 minutes

STEAM: approx. 20 minutes

COOK: 20 minutes

500 ml water, for steaming
cooking spray
3 eggs
100 g almond flour
110 g butter, room temperature
60 g blueberries
1½ tsps. baking powder
120 ml sour cream
130 g swerve
2 tsps. vanilla

1. Pour 500 ml water into the pot. Push in the legs on the Cook & Crisp tray, then place the tray in the bottom position in the pot. Spray Multi-Purpose Tin or 20cm cake tin with cooking spray.
2. Mix all the ingredients in a bowl except blueberries.
3. Pour the batter in the tin and fold in the blueberries.
4. Mix well and transfer the tin on the tray.
5. Close the lid and flip the SmartSwitch to RAPID COOKER. Select STEAM BAKE, set temperature to 180°C, and set time to 20 minutes. Press START/STOP to begin cooking (the unit will steam for approx. 20 minutes, before countdown time begins).
6. When cooking is complete, carefully remove the tin and allow to cool for 5 minutes. Cut into slices to serve.

Beef and Kale Omelette

SERVES: 4

PREP: 15 minutes

TOTAL COOK TIME: 30 minutes

STEAM: approx. 20 minutes

COOK: 10 minutes

250 ml water, for steaming
Cooking spray
225 g leftover beef, coarsely chopped
4 eggs, beaten
65 g kale, torn into pieces and wilted
1 tomato, chopped

2 garlic cloves, pressed
¼ tsp. sugar
60 ml double cream
½ tsp. turmeric powder
Salt and ground black pepper, to taste
⅛ tsp. ground allspice

1. Pour 250 ml water into the pot. Push in the legs on the Cook & Crisp tray, then place the tray in the bottom position in the pot. Spritz four ramekins with cooking spray.
2. Place equal amounts of each of the ingredients into each ramekin and combine well. Arrange the ramekins on the tray.
3. Close the lid and flip the SmartSwitch to RAPID COOKER. Select STEAM BAKE, set temperature to 180°C, and set time to 10 minutes. Press START/STOP to begin cooking (the unit will steam for approx. 20 minutes, before countdown time begins).
4. Carefully remove the ramekins and allow to cool for 5 minutes. Serve immediately.

Pineapple and Chocolate Cake

SERVES: 4

PREP: 10 minutes

TOTAL COOK TIME: 40 minutes

STEAM: approx. 15 minutes

COOK: 25 minutes

500 ml water, for steaming
cooking spray
300 g flour
110 g butter, melted
50 g sugar
225 g pineapple, chopped
120 ml pineapple juice
30 g dark chocolate, grated
1 large egg
30 ml skimmed milk

1. Pour 500 ml water into the pot. Push in the legs on the Cook & Crisp tray, then place the tray in the bottom position in the pot. Spray a cake tin with cooking spray.
2. In a bowl, combine the butter and flour to create a crumbly consistency.
3. Add the sugar, chopped pineapple, juice, and grated dark chocolate and mix well.
4. In a separate bowl, combine the egg and milk. Add this mixture to the flour mixture and stir well until a soft dough forms.
5. Pour the mixture into the cake tin and transfer on the tray.
6. Close the lid and flip the SmartSwitch to RAPID COOKER. Select STEAM BAKE, set temperature to 180°C, and set time to 25 minutes. Press START/STOP to begin cooking (the unit will steam for approx. 15 minutes, before countdown time begins).
7. When cooking is complete, serve immediately.

Cheesy Dinner Rolls

SERVES: 2

PREP: 10 minutes
TOTAL COOK TIME: 12 minutes
STEAM: approx. 4 minutes
COOK: 8 minutes

250 ml water, for steaming
cooking spray
2 dinner rolls
50 g Parmesan cheese, grated
30 g unsalted butter, melted
½ tsp. garlic bread seasoning mix

1. Pour 250 ml water into the pot. Push in the legs on the Cook & Crisp tray, then place the tray in the bottom position in the pot. Spray Multi-Purpose Tin or 20cm cake tin with cooking spray.
2. Cut the dinner rolls in slits and stuff cheese in the slits.
3. Top with butter and garlic bread seasoning mix.
4. Arrange the dinner rolls to the prepared pan, then place the pan on the tray.
5. Close the lid and flip the SmartSwitch to RAPID COOKER. Select STEAM BAKE, set temperature to 180°C, and set time to 8 minutes. Press START/STOP to begin cooking (the unit will steam for approx. 4 minutes, before countdown time begins).
6. When the time is up, dish out in a platter and serve hot.

Courgette and Mushroom Pizza

SERVES: 4

PREP: 20 minutes
TOTAL COOK TIME: 28 minutes
STEAM: approx. 20 minutes
COOK: 8 minutes

250 ml water, for steaming
4 Portobello mushroom caps, stemmed and gills removed
85 g courgette, shredded
2 tbsps. sweet red pepper, seeded and chopped
4 Kalamata olives, sliced
120 g hummus
15 ml balsamic vinegar
Salt and black pepper, to taste
4 tbsps. pasta sauce
1 garlic clove, minced
1 tsp. dried basil

1. Pour 250 ml water into the pot. Push in the legs on the Cook & Crisp tray, then place the tray in the bottom position in the pot. Spray Multi-Purpose Tin or 20cm cake tin with cooking spray.
2. Coat both sides of all Portobello mushroom cap with vinegar.
3. Season the inside of each mushroom cap with salt and black pepper.
4. Divide pasta sauce and garlic inside each mushroom.
5. Arrange mushroom caps in the prepared tin, then place the tin on the tray.
6. Close the lid and flip the SmartSwitch to RAPID COOKER. Select STEAM BAKE, set temperature to 165°C, and set time to 8 minutes. Press START/STOP to begin cooking (the unit will steam for approx. 20 minutes, before countdown time begins).
7. With 4 minutes remaining, open the lid and top courgette, red peppers and olives on each mushroom cap. Season with basil, salt, and black pepper. Close the lid to continue cooking.
8. Dish out in a serving platter. Spread hummus on each mushroom pizza and serve.

Rich Layered Cake

PREP: 15 minutes
TOTAL COOK TIME: 45 minutes
STEAM: approx. 20 minutes
COOK: 25 minutes

500 ml water, for steaming
cooking spray
For the Cake:
1 tsp. ground cinnamon
Pinch of salt
85 g caster sugar
100 g plain flour

100 g butter, softened
2 medium eggs
For the Filling:
50 g butter, softened
30 ml strawberry jam
1 tbsp. whipped cream
75 g icing sugar

1. Pour 500 ml water into the pot. Push in the legs on the Cook & Crisp tray, then place the tray in the bottom position in the pot. Spray a cake tin with cooking spray.
2. Mix flour, cinnamon and salt in a large bowl.
3. Beat together sugar, eggs and butter in another bowl until creamy.
4. Stir in the flour mixture slowly and beat until well combined
5. Transfer the mixture into the cake tin, then place the tin on the tray.
6. Close the lid and flip the SmartSwitch to RAPID COOKER. Select STEAM BAKE, set temperature to 180°C, and set time to 25 minutes. Press START/STOP to begin cooking (the unit will steam for approx. 20 minutes, before countdown time begins).
7. When cooking is complete, remove the cake from the tray and cut the cake in 2 portions.
8. For Filling: Mix butter, cream and icing sugar in a bowl and beat until creamy. Place 1 cake portion in a plate, cut side up and spread jam evenly over cake.
9. Top with the butter mixture and place another cake, cut side down over filling to serve.

Super Moist Chocolate Cake

PREP: 5 minutes
TOTAL COOK TIME: 40 minutes
STEAM: approx. 20 minutes
COOK: 20 minutes

500 ml water, for steaming
cooking spray
45 g plain flour
¼ tsp. baking powder
8 g unsweetened cocoa powder
2 eggs, yolks and whites separated

55 ml milk
40 g castor sugar, divided
30 ml vegetable oil
1 tsp. vanilla extract
⅛ tsp. cream of tartar

1. Pour 500 ml water into the pot. Push in the legs on the Cook & Crisp tray, then place the tray in the bottom position in the pot. Spray a chiffon pan with cooking spray.
2. Mix flour, baking powder and cocoa powder in a bowl.
3. Combine the remaining ingredients in another bowl until well combined.
4. Stir in the flour mixture slowly and pour this mixture into the chiffon pan.
5. Cover with the foil paper and poke some holes in the foil paper.
6. Transfer the chiffon pan on the tray.
7. Close the lid and flip the SmartSwitch to RAPID COOKER. Select STEAM BAKE, set temperature to 165°C, and set time to 20 minutes. Press START/STOP to begin cooking (the unit will steam for approx. 20 minutes, before countdown time begins).
8. With 5 minutes remaining, open the lid and remove the foil. Close the lid to continue cooking.
9. When cooking is complete, cut into slices to serve.

Nutmeg Pumpkin Pudding

PREP: 10 minutes
TOTAL COOK TIME: 30 minutes
STEAM: approx. 20 minutes
COOK: 10 minutes

250 ml water, for steaming
cooking spray
730 g pumpkin purée
45 ml honey
1 tbsp. ginger
1 tbsp. cinnamon

1 tsp. clove
1 tsp. nutmeg
240 ml full-fat cream
2 eggs
200 g caster sugar

1. Pour 250 ml water into the pot. Push in the legs on the Cook & Crisp tray, then place the tray in the bottom position in the pot. Spray Multi-Purpose Tin or 20cm cake tin with cooking spray.
2. In a bowl, stir all the ingredients together to combine.
3. Scrape the mixture into the the prepared tin and transfer the tin on the tray.
4. Close the lid and flip the SmartSwitch to RAPID COOKER. Select STEAM BAKE, set temperature to 200°C, and set time to 10 minutes. Press START/STOP to begin cooking (the unit will steam for approx. 20 minutes, before countdown time begins).
5. Serve warm.

CHAPTER 5
AIR FRY

Cajun Courgette Crisps

SERVES: 4

PREP TIME: 5 minutes
COOK TIME: 12 minutes

2 large courgettes, cut into 0.3mm-thick slices
2 tsps. Cajun seasoning
Cooking spray

1. Push in the legs on the Cook & Crisp tray, then place the tray in the bottom of the pot. Spray the tray with cooking spray.
2. Put the courgette slices in a medium bowl and spray them generously with cooking spray.
3. Sprinkle the Cajun seasoning over the courgette and stir to make sure they are evenly coated with oil and seasoning.
4. Close the lid and flip the SmartSwitch to AIR FRY/HOB. Select AIRFRY, set temperature to 200°C, and set time to 17 minutes (unit will need to preheat for 5 minutes, so set an external timer if desired). Press START/STOP to begin cooking.
5. When the unit is preheated and the time reaches 12 minutes, place the slices on the tray. Close the lid to begin cooking.
6. After 6 minutes, open the lid and flip the slices over with silicone-tipped tongs to ensure even cooking. Close the lid to continue cooking.
7. When cooking is complete, serve immediately.

Old-Fashioned Onion Rings

SERVES: 6

PREP TIME: 10 minutes
COOK TIME: 10 minutes

cooking spray
1 large onion, cut into rings
150 g plain flour
240 ml milk
1 egg
75 g dry bread crumbs
Salt, to taste

1. Push in the legs on the Cook & Crisp tray, then place the tray in the bottom of the pot. Spray the tray with cooking spray.
2. Mix together flour and salt in a dish.
3. Whisk egg with milk in a second dish until well mixed.
4. Place the breadcrumbs in a third dish.
5. Coat the onion rings with the flour mixture and dip into the egg mixture. Lastly dredge in the breadcrumbs.
6. Close the lid and flip the SmartSwitch to AIR FRY/HOB. Select AIRFRY, set temperature to 200°C, and set time to 15 minutes (unit will need to preheat for 5 minutes, so set an external timer if desired). Press START/STOP to begin cooking.
7. When the unit is preheated and the time reaches 10 minutes, place the onion rings on the tray. Close the lid to begin cooking.
8. After 5 minutes, open the lid and flip the onion rings with silicone-tipped tongs to ensure even cooking. Close the lid to continue cooking.
9. When cooking is complete, serve hot.

Herbed Pitta Crisps

SERVES: 4

PREP TIME: 5 minutes
COOK TIME: 5 minutes

¼ tsp. dried basil
¼ tsp. marjoram
¼ tsp. ground oregano
¼ tsp. garlic powder

¼ tsp. ground thyme
¼ tsp. salt
2 whole grain 15-cm pittas
Cooking spray

1. Push in the legs on the Cook & Crisp tray, then place the tray in the bottom of the pot. Spray the tray with cooking spray.
2. Mix all the seasonings together.
3. Cut each pitta half into 4 wedges. Break apart wedges at the fold.
4. Mist one side of pitta wedges with oil. Sprinkle with half of seasoning mix.
5. Turn pita wedges over, mist the other side with oil, and sprinkle with remaining seasonings.
6. Close the lid and flip the SmartSwitch to AIR FRY/HOB. Select AIRFRY, set temperature to 165°C, and set time to 10 minutes (unit will need to preheat for 5 minutes, so set an external timer if desired). Press START/STOP to begin cooking.
7. When the unit is preheated and the time reaches 5 minutes, place the pitta wedges on the tray. Close the lid to begin cooking.
8. After 3 minutes, open the lid and toss the pitta wedges with silicone-tipped tongs to ensure even cooking. Close the lid to continue cooking, until crisp.
9. When cooking is complete, serve hot.

Garlic Scallops

SERVES: 4

PREP: 10 minutes
TOTAL COOK TIME: 13 minutes

Cooking spray
450 g small scallops, patted dry
10 ml olive oil
1 packet dry zesty Italian dressing mix
1 tsp. minced garlic

1. Push in the legs on the Cook & Crisp tray, then place the tray in the bottom of the pot. Spray the tray with cooking spray.
2. In a large zip-top plastic bag, mix the olive oil, Italian dressing mix, and garlic.
3. Place the scallops, seal the zip-top bag, and coat the scallops evenly in the seasoning mixture.
4. Close the lid and flip the SmartSwitch to AIR FRY/HOB. Select AIRFRY, set temperature to 200°C, and set time to 18 minutes (unit will need to preheat for 5 minutes, so set an external timer if desired). Press START/STOP to begin cooking.
5. When the unit is preheated and the time reaches 13 minutes, place the scallops on the tray. Close the lid to begin cooking.
6. After 7 minutes, open the lid and toss the scallops with silicone-tipped tongs to ensure even cooking. Close the lid to continue cooking, until the scallops reach an internal temperature of 50ºC.
7. Serve immediately.

Tortilla Chips

SERVES: 2

PREP TIME: 5 minutes
COOK TIME: 5 minutes

cooking spray
8 corn tortillas
15 ml olive oil
Salt, to taste

1. Push in the legs on the Cook & Crisp tray, then place the tray in the bottom of the pot. Spray the tray with cooking spray.
2. Slice the corn tortillas into triangles. Coat with a light brushing of olive oil.
3. Close the lid and flip the SmartSwitch to AIR FRY/HOB. Select AIRFRY, set temperature to 200°C, and set time to 10 minutes (unit will need to preheat for 5 minutes, so set an external timer if desired). Press START/STOP to begin cooking.
4. When the unit is preheated and the time reaches 5 minutes, place the tortilla pieces on the tray. Close the lid to begin cooking.
5. Season with salt before serving.

Crunchy Chickpeas

SERVES: 4

PREP TIME: 5 minutes
COOK TIME: 15 minutes

cooking spray
1 (425 g) tin chickpeas, rinsed and drained
15 ml olive oil
½ tsp. ground cumin
½ tsp. cayenne pepper
½ tsp. smoked paprika
Salt, taste

1. Push in the legs on the Cook & Crisp tray, then place the tray in the bottom of the pot. Spray the tray with cooking spray.
2. Mix together all the ingredients in a bowl and toss to coat well.
3. Close the lid and flip the SmartSwitch to AIR FRY/HOB. Select AIRFRY, set temperature to 200°C, and set time to 20 minutes (unit will need to preheat for 5 minutes, so set an external timer if desired). Press START/STOP to begin cooking.
4. When the unit is preheated and the time reaches 15 minutes, place the chickpeas on the tray. Close the lid to begin cooking.
5. After 8 minutes, open the lid and toss the chickpeas with silicone-tipped tongs to ensure even cooking. Close the lid to continue cooking.
6. When cooking is complete, serve warm.

Simple Ribeye Steak

SERVES: 1

PREP: 5 minutes
TOTAL COOK TIME: 15 minutes

cooking spray
1 (450 g) ribeye steak
Salt and ground black pepper, to taste
15 ml peanut oil
7 g butter
½ tsp. thyme, chopped

1. Push in the legs on the Cook & Crisp tray, then place the tray in the bottom of the pot. Spray the tray with cooking spray.
2. Season the steaks with salt and pepper. Spritz the steak with peanut oil.
3. Close the lid and flip the SmartSwitch to AIR FRY/HOB. Select AIRFRY, set temperature to 190°C, and set time to 20 minutes (unit will need to preheat for 5 minutes, so set an external timer if desired). Press START/STOP to begin cooking.
4. When the unit is preheated and the time reaches 15 minutes, place the steak on the tray. Close the lid to begin cooking.
5. After 5 minutes, open the lid and flip the steak with silicone-tipped tongs to ensure even cooking. Close the lid to continue cooking. Toss in the butter and thyme when 5 minutes remain.
6. Carefully transfer to a plate, let rest for 5 minutes and serve hot.

Crispy Apple Crisps

SERVES: 1

PREP: 5 minutes
TOTAL COOK TIME: 25 minutes

1 Honeycrisp or Pink Lady apple

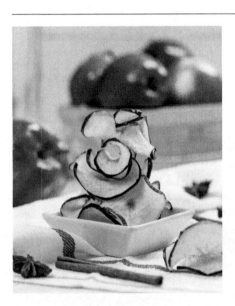

1. Push in the legs on the Cook & Crisp tray, then place the tray in the bottom of the pot. Spray the tray with cooking spray.
2. Core the apple with an apple corer, leaving apple whole. Cut the apple into 3-mm-thick slices.
3. Close the lid and flip the SmartSwitch to AIR FRY/HOB. Select AIRFRY, set temperature to 150°C, and set time to 30 minutes (unit will need to preheat for 5 minutes, so set an external timer if desired). Press START/STOP to begin cooking.
4. When the unit is preheated and the time reaches 25 minutes, place the apple slices on the tray. Close the lid to begin cooking.
5. Open the lid and toss the apple with silicone-tipped tongs and rotate them from top to bottom. Close the lid to continue cooking. Repeat this every five time to make an even cooking.
6. Put the apple crisps in a single layer on a wire rack to cool. Apples will become crisper as they cool. Serve at once.

BBQ Pork Steaks

SERVES: 8

PREP: 5 minutes
TOTAL COOK TIME: 15 minutes

cooking spray
4 pork steaks
100 g brown sugar
120 ml ketchup
30 ml BBQ sauce
1 tbsp. Cajun seasoning
15 ml vinegar
5 ml soy sauce

1. Push in the legs on the Cook & Crisp tray, then place the tray in the bottom of the pot. Spray the tray with cooking spray.
2. Scatter pork steaks with Cajun seasoning.
3. Mix remaining ingredients and brush onto steaks.
4. Close the lid and flip the SmartSwitch to AIR FRY/HOB. Select AIRFRY, set temperature to 190°C, and set time to 20 minutes (unit will need to preheat for 5 minutes, so set an external timer if desired). Press START/STOP to begin cooking.
5. When the unit is preheated and the time reaches 15 minutes, place the pork chops on the tray. Close the lid to begin cooking, until just browned.
6. Serve hot.

Mustard Lamb Ribs

SERVES: 4

PREP: 5 minutes
TOTAL COOK TIME: 18 minutes

cooking spray
450 g lamb ribs
30 ml mustard
240 ml Green yogurt
10 g mint leaves, chopped
1 tsp. rosemary, chopped
Salt and ground black pepper, to taste

1. Push in the legs on the Cook & Crisp tray, then place the tray in the bottom of the pot. Spray the tray with cooking spray.
2. Apply the mustard to the lamb ribs with a brush, and season with rosemary, salt, and pepper.
3. Close the lid and flip the SmartSwitch to AIR FRY/HOB. Select AIRFRY, set temperature to 180°C, and set time to 23 minutes (unit will need to preheat for 5 minutes, so set an external timer if desired). Press START/STOP to begin cooking.
4. When the unit is preheated and the time reaches 18 minutes, place the lamb ribs on the tray. Close the lid to begin cooking.
5. Meanwhile, mix the mint leaves and yogurt in a bowl.
6. Remove the lamb ribs to a plate and serve hot with the mint yogurt.

Crispy Breaded Olives

SERVES: 4

PREP TIME: 5 minutes COOK TIME: 8 minutes	1 (160-g) jar pitted green olives 65 g plain flour 45 g bread crumbs 1 egg Cooking spray

1. Push in the legs on the Cook & Crisp tray, then place the tray in the bottom of the pot. Spray the tray with cooking spray.
2. Remove the olives from the jar and dry thoroughly with paper towels.
3. In a small bowl, combine the flour with salt and pepper to taste. Place the bread crumbs in another small bowl. In a third small bowl, beat the egg.
4. Dip the olives in the flour, then the egg, and then the bread crumbs.
5. Close the lid and flip the SmartSwitch to AIR FRY/HOB. Select AIRFRY, set temperature to 200°C, and set time to 13 minutes (unit will need to preheat for 5 minutes, so set an external timer if desired). Press START/STOP to begin cooking.
6. When the unit is preheated and the time reaches 8 minutes, place the breaded olives on the tray. Spray the olives with cooking spray. Close the lid to begin cooking.
7. With 2 minutes remaining, open the lid and flip the olives with silicone-tipped tongs to ensure even cooking. Close the lid to continue cooking.
8. Cool before serving.

Homemade Chicken Fajitas

SERVES: 4

PREP: 15 minutes TOTAL COOK TIME: 15 minutes	cooking spray 4 (140-g) low-sodium boneless, skinless chicken breasts, cut into 10x1 cm strips 2 red bell peppers, sliced 250 g grape tomatoes, sliced 80 ml nonfat sour cream 4 low-sodium whole-wheat tortillas 15 ml freshly squeezed lemon juice 10 ml olive oil 2 tsps. chilli powder

1. Push in the legs on the Cook & Crisp tray, then place the tray in the bottom of the pot. Spray the tray with cooking spray.
2. In a large bowl, combine the chicken, lemon juice, olive oil, and chilli powder. Toss to coat well.
3. Close the lid and flip the SmartSwitch to AIR FRY/HOB. Select AIRFRY, set temperature to 200°C, and set time to 20 minutes (unit will need to preheat for 5 minutes, so set an external timer if desired). Press START/STOP to begin cooking.
4. When the unit is preheated and the time reaches 15 minutes, place the chicken on the tray. Close the lid to begin cooking, until the chicken reaches an internal temperature of 75°C on a meat thermometer.
5. Assemble the fajitas with the tortillas, chicken, bell peppers, tomatoes and sour cream. Serve hot.

Barbecue Chicken

SERVES: 8

PREP: 10 minutes

TOTAL COOK TIME: 18-20 minutes

cooking spray
4 (140-g) low-sodium boneless, skinless chicken breasts
1 red chilli, minced
2 garlic cloves, minced
80 ml no-salt-added tomato sauce
30 ml low-sodium grainy mustard
30 ml apple cider vinegar
15 ml honey
3 tbsps. minced onion

1. Push in the legs on the Cook & Crisp tray, then place the tray in the bottom of the pot. Spray the tray with cooking spray.
2. In a small bowl, toss together the tomato sauce, mustard, cider vinegar, garlic, red chilli, honey, and onion.
3. Brush the chicken breasts with some sauce.
4. Close the lid and flip the SmartSwitch to AIR FRY/HOB. Select AIRFRY, set temperature to 200°C, and set time to 20 minutes (unit will need to preheat for 5 minutes, so set an external timer if desired). Press START/STOP to begin cooking.
5. When the unit is preheated and the time reaches 18 minutes, place the chicken on the tray. Close the lid to begin cooking.
6. After 10 minutes, open the lid. Turn the chicken over and brush with more sauce. Close the lid to continue cooking.
7. Turn the chicken again; brush with more sauce. Cook for 3 to 5 minutes more, or until the chicken reaches an internal temperature of 74°C on a meat thermometer. Discard any remaining sauce. Serve hot.

Butter Apple Roll-Ups

MAKES: 8 ROLL-UPS

PREP TIME: 5 minutes

COOK TIME: 6 minutes

cooking spray
8 slices whole wheat sandwich bread
115 g cheddar cheese, grated
½ small apple, chopped
30 g butter, melted

1. Push in the legs on the Cook & Crisp tray, then place the tray in the bottom of the pot. Spray the tray with cooking spray.
2. Remove the crusts from the bread and flatten the slices with a rolling pin. Don't be gentle. Press hard so that bread will be very thin.
3. Top bread slices with cheese and chopped apple, dividing the ingredients evenly.
4. Roll up each slice tightly and secure each with one or two toothpicks.
5. Brush outside of rolls with melted butter.
6. Close the lid and flip the SmartSwitch to AIR FRY/HOB. Select AIRFRY, set temperature to 200°C, and set time to 11 minutes (unit will need to preheat for 5 minutes, so set an external timer if desired). Press START/STOP to begin cooking.
7. When the unit is preheated and the time reaches 6 minutes, place the roll-ups on the tray. Close the lid to begin cooking, until outside is crisp and nicely browned.
8. Serve hot.

Tropical Fruit Sticks

PREP TIME: 5 minutes
COOK TIME: 10 minutes

cooking spray
½ fresh pineapple, cut into sticks
25 g desiccated coconut

1. Push in the legs on the Cook & Crisp tray, then place the tray in the bottom of the pot. Spray the tray with cooking spray.
2. Coat the pineapple sticks in the desiccated coconut.
3. Close the lid and flip the SmartSwitch to AIR FRY/HOB. Select AIRFRY, set temperature to 180°C, and set time to 15 minutes (unit will need to preheat for 5 minutes, so set an external timer if desired). Press START/STOP to begin cooking.
4. When the unit is preheated and the time reaches 10 minutes, place the pineapple sticks on the tray. Close the lid to begin cooking.
5. After 5 minutes, open the lid and flip the pineapple sticks with silicone-tipped tongs to ensure even cooking. Close the lid to continue cooking.
6. When cooking is complete, serve immediately.

CHAPTER 6
BAKE/ROAST

Turkey Breast with Herb

SERVES: 6

PREP TIME: 20 minutes
COOK TIME: 40 minutes

Cooking spray
15 ml olive oil
2 garlic cloves, minced
2 tsps. Dijon mustard
1½ tsps. rosemary

1½ tsps. sage
1½ tsps. thyme
1 tsp. salt
½ tsp. freshly ground black pepper
1.4 kg turkey breast, thawed if frozen

1. Push in the legs on the Cook & Crisp tray, then place the tray in the bottom of the pot. Spray the tray with cooking spray.
2. In a small bowl, mix together the garlic, olive oil, Dijon mustard, rosemary, sage, thyme, salt, and pepper to make a paste. Smear the paste all over the turkey breast.
3. Close the lid and flip the SmartSwitch to AIR FRY/HOB. Select BAKE & ROAST, set temperature to 200°C, and set time to 45 minutes (unit will need to preheat for 5 minutes, so set an external timer if desired). Press START/STOP to begin cooking.
4. When the unit is preheated and the time reaches 40 minutes, place the turkey breast on the tray. Close the lid to begin cooking.
5. After 20 minutes, open the lid. Flip turkey breast over and baste it with any drippings that have collected in the bottom of the pot. Close the lid to continue cooking, until the internal temperature of the meat reaches at least 77°C.
6. When cooking is complete, let the turkey rest for 10 minutes before slicing and serving.

Lemon Pork Tenderloin

SERVES: 4 TO 6

PREP TIME: 10 minutes
COOK TIME: 30 minutes

cooking spray
60 ml olive oil
60 ml soy sauce
60 ml freshly squeezed lemon juice
1 garlic clove, minced

1 tbsp. Dijon mustard
1 tsp. salt
½ tsp. freshly ground black pepper
900 g pork tenderloin

1. Push in the legs on the Cook & Crisp tray, then place the tray in the bottom of the pot. Spray the tray with cooking spray.
2. In a large mixing bowl, make the marinade: Mix the olive oil, soy sauce, lemon juice, minced garlic, Dijon mustard, salt, and pepper. Reserve 60 ml of the marinade.
3. Put the tenderloin in a large bowl and pour the remaining marinade over the meat. Cover and marinate in the refrigerator for about 1 hour.
4. Close the lid and flip the SmartSwitch to AIR FRY/HOB. Select BAKE & ROAST, set temperature to 190°C, and set time to 35 minutes (unit will need to preheat for 5 minutes, so set an external timer if desired). Press START/STOP to begin cooking.
5. When the unit is preheated and the time reaches 30 minutes, place the marinated pork tenderloin on the tray. Close the lid to begin cooking.
6. With 20 minutes remaining, open the lid. Flip the pork and baste it with half of the reserved marinade. Close the lid to continue cooking. Repeat this process when 10 minutes remain.
7. When cooking is complete, serve hot.

Garlic Soy Chicken Thighs

SERVES: 2

PREP : 10 minutes
TOTAL COOK TIME: 25 minutes

cooking spray
2 bone-in, skin-on chicken thighs (200-230 g each)
4 garlic cloves, smashed and peeled
30 ml chicken stock

30 ml reduced-sodium soy sauce
20 g caster sugar
2 large scallions, cut into 5-7.5 cm batons, plus more, thinly sliced, for garnish

1. Push in the legs on the Cook & Crisp tray, then place the tray in the bottom of the pot. Spray the tray with cooking spray.
2. Combine the chicken stock, soy sauce, and sugar in the pan and stir until the sugar dissolves. Place the garlic cloves, scallions, and chicken thighs, turning the thighs to coat them evenly in the marinade, then resting them skin-side up.
3. Close the lid and flip the SmartSwitch to AIR FRY/HOB. Select BAKE & ROAST, set temperature to 200°C, and set time to 30 minutes (unit will need to preheat for 5 minutes, so set an external timer if desired). Press START/STOP to begin cooking.
4. When the unit is preheated and the time reaches 25 minutes, place the chicken thighs on the tray. Close the lid to begin cooking, flipping the thighs every 5 minutes after the first 10 minutes, until the thighs are cooked through and the marinade is reduced to a sticky glaze over the chicken.
5. Transfer the tray and serve the chicken thighs warm, with any remaining glaze spooned over top and scattered with more sliced scallions.

Panko Salmon Patties

SERVES: 4

PREP : 10 minutes
TOTAL COOK TIME: 10 minutes

Cooking spray
2 (210 g) tins of salmon, flaked
2 large eggs, beaten
80 g panko bread crumbs

50 g minced onion
1½ tsps. Italian herb seasoning
1 tsp. garlic powder

1. Push in the legs on the Cook & Crisp tray, then place the tray in the bottom of the pot. Line the tray with parchment paper.
2. Stir together the salmon, eggs, and onion in a medium bowl.
3. Whisk the bread crumbs, Italian herb seasoning, and garlic powder in a small bowl until blended well. Place the bread crumb mixture to the salmon mixture and stir well until blended. Form the mixture into 8 patties.
4. Close the lid and flip the SmartSwitch to AIR FRY/HOB. Select BAKE & ROAST, set temperature to 180°C, and set time to 15 minutes (unit will need to preheat for 5 minutes, so set an external timer if desired). Press START/STOP to begin cooking.
5. When the unit is preheated and the time reaches 10 minutes, place half the patties on the tray, working in batches. Close the lid to begin cooking.
6. After 5 minutes, open the lid. Flip the patties over and lightly spritz with cooking spray. Close the lid to continue cooking, until browned and firm.
7. Serve hot.

Honey-Roasted Pears with Walnuts

SERVES: 4

PREP TIME: 5 minutes
COOK TIME: 20 minutes

cooking spray
2 large Conference pears, halved and deseeded
45 ml honey
15 g unsalted butter
½ tsp. ground cinnamon
25 g walnuts, chopped
25 g part skim low-fat ricotta cheese, divided

1. Push in the legs on the Cook & Crisp tray, then place the tray in the bottom of the pot. Spray Multi-Purpose Tin or 20cm cake tin with cooking spray.
2. Place the pears, cut side up on the tin.
3. In a small microwave-safe bowl, melt the honey, butter, and cinnamon. Brush this mixture over the cut sides of the pears.
4. Pour 45 ml water around the pears in the tin.
5. Close the lid and flip the SmartSwitch to AIR FRY/HOB. Select BAKE & ROAST, set temperature to 180°C, and set time to 25 minutes (unit will need to preheat for 5 minutes, so set an external timer if desired). Press START/STOP to begin cooking.
6. When the unit is preheated and the time reaches 20 minutes, place the tin on the tray. Close the lid to begin cooking, until tender, basting once with the liquid in the pan.
7. Carefully remove the pears from the tin and place on a serving plate. Drizzle each with some liquid from the tin, sprinkle the walnuts on top, and serve with a spoonful of ricotta cheese.

Beef Cheeseburgers

SERVES: 2

PREP TIME: 15 minutes
COOK TIME: 12 minutes

cooking spray
225 g minced beef
2 tbsps. fresh coriander, minced
2 slices cheddar cheese
2 salad leaves
2 dinner rolls, cut into half
1 garlic clove, minced
Salt and black pepper, to taste

1. Push in the legs on the Cook & Crisp tray, then place the tray in the bottom of the pot. Spray the tray with cooking spray.
2. Mix the beef, garlic, coriander, salt, and black pepper in a bowl.
3. Make 2 equal-sized patties from the beef mixture.
4. Close the lid and flip the SmartSwitch to AIR FRY/HOB. Select BAKE & ROAST, set temperature to 180°C, and set time to 17 minutes (unit will need to preheat for 5 minutes, so set an external timer if desired). Press START/STOP to begin cooking.
5. When the unit is preheated and the time reaches 12 minutes, place the patties on the tray. Close the lid to begin cooking.
6. With 1 minute remaining, open the lid and top each patty with 1 cheese slice. Close the lid to continue cooking.
7. Dish out in a platter. Place dinner rolls in a serving platter and arrange salad leaf between each dinner roll. Top with 1 patty and immediately serve.

Leg of Lamb with Brussels Sprouts

SERVES: 6

PREP TIME: 20 minutes
COOK TIME: 35 minutes

cooking spray
1 kg leg of lamb
1 tbsp. fresh rosemary, minced
1 tbsp. fresh lemon thyme
680 g Brussels sprouts, trimmed
45 ml olive oil, divided
1 garlic clove, minced
Salt and ground black pepper, as required
30 ml honey

1. Push in the legs on the Cook & Crisp tray, then place the tray in the bottom of the pot. Spray the tray with cooking spray.
2. Make slits in the leg of lamb with a sharp knife.
3. Mix 30 ml oil, herbs, garlic, salt, and black pepper in a bowl.
4. Coat the leg of lamb with oil mixture generously.
5. Close the lid and flip the SmartSwitch to AIR FRY/HOB. Select BAKE & ROAST, set temperature to 190°C, and set time to 40 minutes (unit will need to preheat for 5 minutes, so set an external timer if desired). Press START/STOP to begin cooking.
6. When the unit is preheated and the time reaches 35 minutes, place the leg of lamb on the tray. Close the lid to begin cooking.
7. After 20 minutes, open the lid. Coat the Brussels sprouts evenly with the remaining oil and honey and arrange them on the tray. Close the lid to continue cooking.
8. When cooking is complete, dish out to serve warm.

Sweet Beef and Mango Skewers

SERVES: 4

PREP TIME: 10 minutes
COOK TIME: 8 minutes

340 g beef sirloin tip, cut into 2.5 cm cubes
30 ml balsamic vinegar
15 ml olive oil
15 ml honey

½ tsp. dried marjoram
Pinch of salt
Freshly ground black pepper, to taste
1 mango

1. Push in the legs on the Cook & Crisp tray, then place the tray in the bottom of the pot. Spray the tray with cooking spray.
2. Put the beef cubes in a medium bowl and add the balsamic vinegar, olive oil, honey, marjoram, salt, and pepper. Mix well, then massage the marinade into the beef with your hands. Set aside.
3. To prepare the mango, stand it on end and cut the skin off, using a sharp knife. Then carefully cut around the oval pit to remove the flesh. Cut the mango into 2.5 cm cubes.
4. Thread metal skewers alternating with three beef cubes and two mango cubes.
5. Close the lid and flip the SmartSwitch to AIR FRY/HOB. Select BAKE & ROAST, set temperature to 200°C, and set time to 13 minutes (unit will need to preheat for 5 minutes, so set an external timer if desired). Press START/STOP to begin cooking.
6. When the unit is preheated and the time reaches 8 minutes, place the skewers on the tray. Close the lid to begin cooking.
7. When cooking is complete, serve hot.

Lush Vegetables Roast

PREP: 15 minutes

TOTAL COOK TIME: 17 minutes

300 g small parsnips, peeled and cubed
300 g celery, sliced
300 g small butternut squash, cut in half, deseeded and cubed
2 red onions, sliced
1 tbsp. fresh thyme needles
15 ml olive oil
Salt and ground black pepper, to taste

1. Push in the legs on the Cook & Crisp tray, then place the tray in the bottom of the pot. Spray the tray with cooking spray.
2. Combine the cut vegetables with the thyme, olive oil, salt and pepper.
3. Close the lid and flip the SmartSwitch to AIR FRY/HOB. Select BAKE & ROAST, set temperature to 200°C, and set time to 22 minutes (unit will need to preheat for 5 minutes, so set an external timer if desired). Press START/STOP to begin cooking.
4. When the unit is preheated and the time reaches 17 minutes, place the vegetables on the tray. Close the lid to begin cooking.
5. After 10 minutes, open the lid and toss the vegetables with silicone-tipped tongs to ensure even cooking. Close the lid to continue cooking.
6. When cooking is complete, serve warm.

Honey Cod with Sesame Seeds

PREP: 5 minutes

TOTAL COOK TIME: 10 minutes

Cooking spray
170 g fresh cod fillet
15 ml reduced-sodium soy sauce
10 ml honey
1 tsp. sesame seeds

1. Push in the legs on the Cook & Crisp tray, then place the tray in the bottom of the pot. Spray the tray with cooking spray.
2. In a small bowl, mix the soy sauce and honey.
3. Close the lid and flip the SmartSwitch to AIR FRY/HOB. Select BAKE & ROAST, set temperature to 200°C, and set time to 15 minutes (unit will need to preheat for 5 minutes, so set an external timer if desired). Press START/STOP to begin cooking.
4. When the unit is preheated and the time reaches 10 minutes, place the cod on the tray, brush with the soy mixture, and sprinkle sesame seeds on top. Close the lid to begin cooking, until opaque.
5. Transfer the fish and let cool on a wire rack for 5 minutes before serving.

Doughnuts Pudding

SERVES: 4

PREP TIME: 15 minutes
COOK TIME: 50 minutes

cooking spray
6 glazed doughnuts, cut into small pieces
130 g frozen sweet cherries
75 g sultanas
90 g semi-sweet chocolate baking chips
4 egg yolks
50 g caster sugar
1 tsp. ground cinnamon
360 ml whipping cream

1. Push in the legs on the Cook & Crisp tray, then place the tray in the bottom of the pot. Spray Multi-Purpose Tin or 20cm cake tin with cooking spray.
2. Mix doughnut pieces, cherries, sultanas, chocolate chips, sugar, and cinnamon in a large bowl.
3. Whisk the egg yolks with whipping cream in another bowl until well combined.
4. Combine the egg yolk mixture into the doughnut mixture and mix well.
5. Arrange the doughnuts mixture evenly into the tin.
6. Close the lid and flip the SmartSwitch to AIR FRY/HOB. Select BAKE & ROAST, set temperature to 160°C, and set time to 55 minutes (unit will need to preheat for 5 minutes, so set an external timer if desired). Press START/STOP to begin cooking.
7. When the unit is preheated and the time reaches 50 minutes, place the tin on the tray. Close the lid to begin cooking.
8. Serve warm.

Beef Roast

SERVES: 6

PREP TIME: 10 minutes
COOK TIME: 30 minutes

cooking spray
1.1 kg beef eye of round roast, trimmed
30 ml olive oil
½ tsp. onion powder
½ tsp. garlic powder
½ tsp. cayenne pepper
½ tsp. ground black pepper
Salt, to taste

1. Push in the legs on the Cook & Crisp tray, then place the tray in the bottom of the pot. Spray the tray with cooking spray.
2. Rub the roast generously with all the spices and coat with olive oil.
3. Close the lid and flip the SmartSwitch to AIR FRY/HOB. Select BAKE & ROAST, set temperature to 200°C, and set time to 35 minutes (unit will need to preheat for 5 minutes, so set an external timer if desired). Press START/STOP to begin cooking.
4. When the unit is preheated and the time reaches 30 minutes, place the roast on the tray. Close the lid to begin cooking.
5. After 15 minutes, open the lid and flip the roast with silicone-tipped tongs to ensure even cooking. Close the lid to continue cooking.
6. When cooking is complete, dish out the roast and cover with foil.
7. Cut into desired size slices and serve.

Citrus Roasted Pork

PREP TIME: 10 minutes
COOK TIME: 35 minutes

15 ml lime juice
1 tbsp. orange marmalade
1 tsp. coarse brown mustard
1 tsp. curry powder
1 tsp. dried lemongrass
900 g boneless pork loin roast
Salt and ground black pepper, to taste
Cooking spray

1. Push in the legs on the Cook & Crisp tray, then place the tray in the bottom of the pot. Spray the tray with cooking spray.
2. Mix the lime juice, marmalade, mustard, curry powder, and lemongrass.
3. Rub mixture all over the surface of the pork loin. Season with salt and pepper.
4. Close the lid and flip the SmartSwitch to AIR FRY/HOB. Select BAKE & ROAST, set temperature to 190°C, and set time to 40 minutes (unit will need to preheat for 5 minutes, so set an external timer if desired). Press START/STOP to begin cooking.
5. When the unit is preheated and the time reaches 35 minutes, place the pork roast diagonally on the tray. Close the lid to begin cooking.
6. After 20 minutes, open the lid and flip the pork roast with silicone-tipped tongs to ensure even cooking. Close the lid to continue cooking, until the internal temperature reaches at least 63°C.
7. Wrap roast in foil and let rest for 10 minutes before slicing.

BBQ Pork Ribs

PREP TIME: 5 minutes
COOK TIME: 30 minutes

cooking spray
12 g dark brown sugar
7 g sweet paprika
15 g coarse salt
2 g garlic powder
2 g onion powder

2 g poultry seasoning
1 g mustard powder
1 g freshly ground black pepper
1 kg individually cut St. Louis–style pork spareribs

1. Push in the legs on the Cook & Crisp tray, then place the tray in the bottom of the pot. Spray the tray with cooking spray.
2. In a large bowl, whisk together the salt, brown sugar, paprika, garlic powder, onion powder, poultry seasoning, mustard powder, and pepper. Add the ribs and toss. Rub the seasonings into them with your hands until they're fully coated.
3. Close the lid and flip the SmartSwitch to AIR FRY/HOB. Select BAKE & ROAST, set temperature to 190°C, and set time to 35 minutes (unit will need to preheat for 5 minutes, so set an external timer if desired). Press START/STOP to begin cooking.
4. When the unit is preheated and the time reaches 30 minutes, place the ribs on the tray, standing up on their ends and leaned up against the wall of the pot and each other. Close the lid to begin cooking.
5. Transfer the ribs to plates and serve hot.

Herbed Lamb Chops

SERVES: 2

PREP TIME: 10 minutes
COOK TIME: 15 minutes

cooking spray
4 (115 g each) lamb chops
15 ml fresh lemon juice
15 ml olive oil
1 tsp. dried rosemary
1 tsp. dried thyme
1 tsp. dried oregano
½ tsp. ground cumin
½ tsp. ground coriander
Salt and black pepper, to taste

1. Push in the legs on the Cook & Crisp tray, then place the tray in the bottom of the pot. Spray the tray with cooking spray.
2. Mix the lemon juice, oil, herbs, and spices in a large bowl.
3. Coat the chops generously with the herb mixture and refrigerate to marinate for about 1 hour.
4. Close the lid and flip the SmartSwitch to AIR FRY/HOB. Select BAKE & ROAST, set temperature to 200°C, and set time to 20 minutes (unit will need to preheat for 5 minutes, so set an external timer if desired). Press START/STOP to begin cooking.
5. When the unit is preheated and the time reaches 15 minutes, place the chops on the tray. Close the lid to begin cooking.
6. After 5 minutes, open the lid and flip the chops with silicone-tipped tongs to ensure even cooking. Close the lid to continue cooking.
7. When cooking is complete, serve hot.

CHAPTER 7
SEAR/SAUTÉ

Pork and Brussels Sprouts with Oyster Sauce

SERVES: 4

PREP TIME: 12 minutes
COOK TIME: 5 minutes

450 g pork, minced
12 Brussels sprouts, trimmed and halved
1 medium onion, diced
60 ml oyster sauce
60 ml honey
2 garlic cloves, crushed and chopped
30 ml cooking oil
1 tbsp. ginger, crushed and chopped

1. Before getting started, be sure to remove the Cook & Crisp tray from the pot.
2. Flip the SmartSwitch to AIR FRY/HOB. Select SEAR/SAUTÉ and set to HI-5. Press START/STOP to begin cooking.
3. Heat the cooking oil in the pot until it shimmers.
4. Add the garlic, ginger and brussels sprouts and sear for about 1 minute.
5. Place the pork, onion and honey and sauté for about 2 minutes.
6. Add the oyster sauce and toss for about 30 seconds.
7. Serve warm.

Whangarei Style Mussels

SERVES: 4

PREP TIME: 20 minutes
COOK TIME: 25 minutes

450 g mussels, cleaned and debearded
15 ml olive oil
90 g chopped spring onions
2 tbsps. minced garlic
2 tbsps. minced shallots
10 g capers
700 ml tinned tomato sauce
1 tbsp. Italian seasoning
½ tsp. red pepper flakes

1. Before getting started, be sure to remove the Cook & Crisp tray from the pot.
2. Flip the SmartSwitch to AIR FRY/HOB. Select SEAR/SAUTÉ and set to 4. Press START/STOP to begin cooking.
3. Heat the oil and butter in the pot. Sauté the shallots, garlic and capers for about 5 minutes.
4. Stir in the Italian herbs, tomato sauce and red pepper flakes and set to 2.
5. Simmer, covered for about 10 minutes.
6. Stir in the mussels and set to 4.
7. Cook, covered for about 10 minutes.
8. Discard any unopened mussels from the pot.
9. Serve with a garnishing of the spring onions.

Mongolian Beef

SERVES: 4

PREP TIME: 15 minutes

COOK TIME: 10 minutes

30 ml Shaoxing rice wine
15 ml dark soy sauce
1 tbsp. cornflour
340 g flank steak, cut against the grain into 0.5-cm-thick slices
60 ml low-sodium chicken broth
12 g light brown sugar
240 ml vegetable oil
4 or 5 whole dried red Chinese chilies
4 garlic cloves, coarsely chopped
1 tsp. peeled finely minced fresh ginger
½ yellow onion, thinly sliced
6 g coarsely chopped fresh coriander

1. Before getting started, be sure to remove the Cook & Crisp tray from the pot.
2. In a mixing bowl, stir together the rice wine, dark soy, and cornflour. Add the sliced flank steak and toss to coat. Set aside and marinate for 10 minutes.
3. Flip the SmartSwitch to AIR FRY/HOB. Select SEAR/SAUTÉ and set to 4. Press START/STOP to begin cooking.
4. Pour the oil into the pot and bring it to 190°C. You can tell the oil is at the right temperature when you dip the end of a wooden spoon into the oil. If the oil bubbles and sizzles around it, the oil is ready.
5. Lift the beef from the marinade, reserving the marinade. Add the beef to the oil and sauté for 2 to 3 minutes, until it develops a golden crust. Using a skimmer, transfer the beef to a clean bowl and set aside. Add the chicken broth and brown sugar to the marinade bowl and stir to combine.
6. Pour out all but 15 ml oil from the pot. Add the chili peppers, garlic, and ginger. Allow the aromatics to sizzle in the oil for about 10 seconds, swirling gently.
7. Add the onion and sear for 1 to 2 minutes, or until the onion is soft and translucent. Add the chicken broth mixture and toss to combine. Simmer for about 2 minutes, then add the beef and toss everything together for another 30 seconds.
8. Transfer to a platter, garnish with the coriander, and serve hot.

Hoisin Pork

SERVES: 4

PREP TIME: 15 minutes

COOK TIME: 6 minutes

10 ml Shaoxing rice wine
10 ml light soy sauce
½ tsp. chilli paste
340 g boneless pork loin, thinly sliced into julienne strips
30 ml vegetable oil
4 peeled fresh ginger slices, each about the size of a quarter
coarse salt
110 g snow peas, thinly sliced on the diagonal
30 ml hoisin sauce
15 ml water

1. Before getting started, be sure to remove the Cook & Crisp tray from the pot.
2. In a bowl, stir together the rice wine, light soy, and chilli paste. Add the pork and toss to coat. Set aside to marinate for 10 minutes.
3. Flip the SmartSwitch to AIR FRY/HOB. Select SEAR/SAUTÉ and set to 4. Press START/STOP to begin cooking.
4. Pour in the vegetable oil in the pot. Season the oil by adding the ginger and a pinch of salt. Allow the ginger to sizzle in the oil for about 30 seconds, swirling gently.
5. Add the pork and marinade and sauté for 2 to 3 minutes, until no longer pink. Add the snow peas and sauté for about 1 minute, until tender and translucent. Stir in the hoisin sauce and water to loosen the sauce. Continue to toss and flip for 30 seconds, or until the sauce is heated through and the pork and snow peas are coated.
6. Transfer to a platter and serve hot.

Balsamic Bok Choy

SERVES: 4

PREP TIME: 15 minutes
COOK TIME: 15 minutes

4 heads baby bok choy
30 ml balsamic vinegar
45 ml olive oil
1 dash fresh lemon juice
60 ml water
2 tbsps. capers
1½ tsps. minced garlic
1½ tsps. minced fresh ginger root

1. Before getting started, be sure to remove the Cook & Crisp tray from the pot.
2. Separate the leaves from the stems of the bok choy.
3. Cut the stems into bite-sized chunks and shred the leaves.
4. Flip the SmartSwitch to AIR FRY/HOB. Select SEAR/SAUTÉ and set to 3. Press START/STOP to begin cooking.
5. Heat the olive oil in the pot and sear the bok choy stems for about 3 minutes.
6. Add the water and leaves and cook for about 10 minutes.
7. Stir in the capers, garlic and ginger and sauté for about 1 minute more.
8. Drizzle with the vinegar and lemon juice and press START/STOP to turn off the cooker.
9. Serve immediately.

Drunken Prawns

SERVES: 4

PREP TIME: 30 minutes
COOK TIME: 10 minutes

480 ml Shaoxing rice wine
4 peeled fresh ginger slices, each about the size of a quarter
2 tsps. dried goji berries (optional)
2 tsps. sugar
450 g jumbo prawns, peeled and deveined, tails left on
30 ml vegetable oil
coarse salt
2 tsps. cornflour

1. Before getting started, be sure to remove the Cook & Crisp tray from the pot.
2. In a wide mixing bowl, stir together the rice wine, ginger, goji berries (if using), and sugar until the sugar is dissolved. Add the prawns and cover. Marinate in the refrigerator for 20 to 30 minutes.
3. Flip the SmartSwitch to AIR FRY/HOB. Select SEAR/SAUTÉ and set to 4. Press START/STOP to begin cooking.
4. Pour in the vegetable oil in the pot. Season the oil by adding a small pinch of salt, and swirl gently.
5. Add the prawns and vigorously stir-fry, adding a pinch of salt as you flip and toss the prawns around in the pot. Keep moving the prawns around for about 3 minutes, until they just turn pink.
6. Stir the cornflour into the reserved marinade and pour it over the prawns. Toss the prawns and coat with the marinade. It will thicken into a glossy sauce as it begins to boil, about another 5 minutes more.
7. Transfer the prawns and goji berries to a platter, discard the ginger, and serve hot.

Broccoli and Chicken

SERVES: 4

PREP TIME: 15 minutes
COOK TIME: 15 minutes

15 ml Shaoxing rice wine
10 ml light soy sauce
1 tsp. minced garlic
1 tsp. cornflour
¼ tsp. sugar
340 g boneless, skinless chicken thighs, cut into 5 cm chunks
30 ml vegetable oil

4 peeled fresh ginger slices, about the size of a quarter
coarse salt
450 g broccoli, cut into bite-size florets
30 ml water
Red pepper flakes (optional)
60 ml store-bought black bean sauce

1. Before getting started, be sure to remove the Cook & Crisp tray from the pot.
2. In a small bowl, mix together the rice wine, light soy, garlic, cornflour, and sugar. Add the chicken and marinate for 10 minutes.
3. Flip the SmartSwitch to AIR FRY/HOB. Select SEAR/SAUTÉ and set to 4. Press START/STOP to begin cooking.
4. Pour in the vegetable oil in the pot. Add the ginger and a pinch of salt. Allow the ginger to sizzle for about 30 seconds, swirling gently.
5. Transfer the chicken to the pot, discarding the marinade. Sear the chicken for 4 to 5 minutes, until no longer pink. Add the broccoli, water, and a pinch of red pepper flakes (if using) and sear for 1 minute. Close the lid and cook the broccoli for 6 to 8 minutes, until it is crisp-tender.
6. Stir in the black bean sauce until coated and heated through, about 2 minutes, or until the sauce has thickened slightly and become glossy.
7. Discard the ginger, transfer to a platter, and serve hot.

Classic Kerala Curry

SERVES: 8

PREP TIME: 20 minutes
COOK TIME: 50 minutes

1 (1.4-kg) chicken, cut into pieces
1 tsp. ground black pepper
60 ml vegetable oil
Salt to taste
2 onions, chopped

5 russet potatoes, peeled and cut into 2.5 cm pieces
8 cloves garlic, chopped
30 g mild curry powder
10 g hot curry powder

1. Before getting started, be sure to remove the Cook & Crisp tray from the pot.
2. Flip the SmartSwitch to AIR FRY/HOB. Select SEAR/SAUTÉ and set to 4. Press START/STOP to begin cooking.
3. Add the chicken in the pot and enough water to cover and bring to a boil.
4. Set to 3 and simmer for about 20 minutes.
5. Meanwhile in a large wok, heat the vegetable oil on medium heat and sauté the onion and garlic for about 5 minutes.
6. Stir in both curry powders, black pepper and salt and sauté for about 5 minutes.
7. Transfer the onion mixture into the pot with the chicken.
8. Stir in the potatoes and simmer for about 20 minutes.

Braised Lamb and Cabbage

SERVES: 5

PREP TIME: 7 minutes COOK TIME: 5 minutes	450 g boneless leg of lamb or shoulder, cut into 0.5 cm strips 60 g Napa cabbage, shredded 1 medium onion, diced 60 ml rice vinegar 2 garlic cloves, crushed and chopped 30 ml cooking oil 30 ml soy sauce 25 g brown sugar 15 g cornflour 1 tbsp. ginger, crushed and chopped 1 tsp. red pepper flakes

1. Before getting started, be sure to remove the Cook & Crisp tray from the pot.
2. Whisk together the soy sauce, rice vinegar, brown sugar and cornflour in a small bowl. Keep aside.
3. Flip the SmartSwitch to AIR FRY/HOB. Select SEAR/SAUTÉ and set to Hi-5. Press START/STOP to begin cooking.
4. Heat the cooking oil in the pot until it shimmers.
5. Add the garlic, ginger, lamb, onion and red pepper flakes and sauté for about 2 minutes.
6. Pour in the soy sauce mixture and cabbage and stir until a glaze is formed.
7. Serve warm.

Lime Beef

SERVES: 4

PREP TIME: 8 minutes COOK TIME: 6 minutes	450 g sirloin steak, sliced into 0.5 cm strips 1 chile, cut into 0.5 cm rounds 1 lemongrass heart (the bottom 5 cm of the white inner layers), minced 2 garlic cloves, crushed and chopped 4 scallions, cut into 1 cm pieces Juice of 1 lime 30 ml soy sauce 30 ml coconut oil 12 g brown sugar 1 tbsp. ginger, crushed and chopped 1 tsp. cardamom 1 tsp. Chinese five-spice powder

1. Before getting started, be sure to remove the Cook & Crisp tray from the pot.
2. Flip the SmartSwitch to AIR FRY/HOB. Select SEAR/SAUTÉ and set to HI-5. Press START/STOP to begin cooking.
3. Heat the coconut oil in the pot until it shimmers.
4. Add the garlic, ginger, steak, five-spice powder and cardamom and sauté for about 2 minutes.
5. Place the chile, lime juice, brown sugar, lemongrass and soy sauce and sear for about 2 minutes.
6. Sprinkle with the scallions and serve immediately.

Beef and Sugar Snap with Sha Cha

SERVES: 4

PREP TIME: 9 minutes

COOK TIME: 5 minutes

450 g sirloin steak, sliced into 0.5 cm strips
200 g sugar snap or snow pea pods
1 medium onion, cut into 2.5 cm pieces
60 ml sha cha
1 chile, cut into 0.5 cm circles
4 scallions, cut into 2.5 cm pieces
2 cloves garlic, crushed and chopped
30 ml cooking oil
30 ml soy sauce
30 ml Chinese rice wine
1 tbsp. ginger, crushed and chopped

1. Before getting started, be sure to remove the Cook & Crisp tray from the pot.
2. Flip the SmartSwitch to AIR FRY/HOB. Select SEAR/SAUTÉ and set to HI-5. Press START/STOP to begin cooking.
3. Heat the cooking oil in the pot until it shimmers.
4. Add the garlic, ginger, steak and onion and sauté for 1 minute.
5. Pour the rice wine, soy sauce, sha cha and chile and sauté for 1 minute.
6. Place the pea pods and scallions and sauté for 1 minute.
7. Serve warm.

Thai Coconut Curry Lamb

SERVES: 5

PREP TIME: 8 minutes

COOK TIME: 5 minutes

450 g boneless lamb leg or shoulder, cut into 2.5 cm pieces
200 g chopped bok choy
115 g mushrooms, sliced
60 ml tinned coconut milk
1 medium onion, cut into 2.5 cm pieces
1 bird's eye chile, thinly sliced
2 garlic cloves, crushed and chopped
30 ml coconut oil
1 tbsp. red Thai curry paste
1 tbsp. ginger, crushed and chopped
15 g brown sugar
15 ml fish sauce
8 g cornflour

1. Before getting started, be sure to remove the Cook & Crisp tray from the pot.
2. Whisk together the curry paste, coconut milk, brown sugar, fish sauce and cornflour in a small bowl. Keep aside.
3. Flip the SmartSwitch to AIR FRY/HOB. Select SEAR/SAUTÉ and set to HI-5. Press START/STOP to begin cooking.
4. Heat the coconut oil in the pot until it shimmers.
5. Add the garlic, ginger and lamb and sear for about 1 minute.
6. Place the mushrooms, onion and bird's eye chile and sauté for about 1 minute.
7. Put the bok choy and sauté for about 30 seconds.
8. Toss the curry paste mixture and stir until a glaze is formed.
9. Serve warm.

Pork and Carrot with Scallion

SERVES: 4

PREP TIME: 8 minutes
COOK TIME: 5 minutes

450 g pork tenderloin, cut into 2.5 cm pieces
1 medium carrot, roll-cut into 1 cm pieces
1 medium onion, cut into 2.5 cm pieces
1 medium red bell pepper, cut into 2.5 cm pieces
4 scallions, cut into 2.5 cm pieces
2 garlic cloves, crushed and chopped
30 ml cooking oil
20 g sesame seeds
30 ml soy sauce
30 ml honey
1 tbsp. cornflour
1 tbsp. ginger, crushed and chopped
5 ml hot sesame oil

1. Before getting started, be sure to remove the Cook & Crisp tray from the pot.
2. Flip the SmartSwitch to AIR FRY/HOB. Select SEAR/SAUTÉ and set to HI-5. Press START/STOP to begin cooking.
3. Heat the cooking oil in the pot until it shimmers.
4. Add the garlic, ginger and carrot and sear for about 1 minute.
5. Place the pork and sauté for about 1 minute.
6. Then put the onion and bell pepper and sauté for about 1 minute.
7. Pour the sesame oil, honey, soy sauce and cornflour and stir until a light glaze is formed.
8. Sprinkle with the sesame seeds and scallions. Serve warm.

Lemongrass Chicken and Bok Choy

SERVES: 5

PREP TIME: 12 minutes
COOK TIME: 5 minutes

450 g boneless chicken thighs, cut into 2.5 cm pieces
2 heads baby bok choy, leaves separated
110 g sliced mushrooms
1 medium red onion, cut into 2.5 cm pieces
1 medium red bell pepper, cut into 2.5 cm pieces
2 lemongrass hearts (the bottom 5-cm of the white inner layers), finely minced
2 garlic cloves, crushed and chopped
30 ml cooking oil
1 tbsp. ginger, crushed and chopped
1 tsp. fish sauce
5 ml hot sesame oil
Fresh chopped herbs, such as coriander, mint, or parsley, for garnish

1. Before getting started, be sure to remove the Cook & Crisp tray from the pot.
2. Flip the SmartSwitch to AIR FRY/HOB. Select SEAR/SAUTÉ and set to HI-5. Press START/STOP to begin cooking.
3. Heat the cooking oil in the pot until it shimmers.
4. Add the garlic, ginger, lemongrass, and chicken and sear for about 1 minute.
5. Place the onion, mushrooms and bell pepper sauté for about 1 minute.
6. Toss the bok choy, sesame oil and fish sauce and sauté for about 30 seconds.
7. Sprinkle with chopped herbs of your choice and serve warm.

Beans Caprese

PREP TIME: 15 minutes
COOK TIME: 12 minutes

680 g green beans
15 g butter
240 g cherry tomatoes, halved
¾ tsp. garlic salt
12 g sugar
½ tsp. dried basil
Salt and pepper

1. Before getting started, be sure to remove the Cook & Crisp tray from the pot.
2. Flip the SmartSwitch to AIR FRY/HOB. Select SEAR/SAUTÉ and set to HI-5. Press START/STOP to begin cooking.
3. Add water in the pot and heat it until it starts boiling.
4. Sear the green beans for 7 minutes until they become tender. Drain them.
5. Set to 4 and heat the butter until it melts.
6. Sauté the garlic salt, sugar, basil, salt and pepper with cherry tomatoes for 3 minutes.
7. Stir in the green beans and cook for another 2 minutes.
8. Serve your green beans warm.

CHAPTER 8
SLOW COOK

Roast Pork with Red Cabbage

SERVES: 6 TO 8

PREP TIME: 20 minutes
COOK TIME: 9 hours

1 (1.4-kg) pork loin roast
1 large head red cabbage, chopped
2 medium pears, peeled and chopped
2 red onions, chopped
250 ml chicken stock
60 ml apple cider vinegar
4 garlic cloves, minced
45 ml honey
1 tsp. dried thyme leaves
½ tsp. salt

1. Before getting started, be sure to remove the Cook & Crisp tray.
2. Mix the cabbage, onions, pears, and garlic in the bottom of the pot.
3. In a small bowl, mix the vinegar, honey, chicken stock, thyme, and salt, and pour the mixture into the pot.
4. Place the pork on top, nestling the meat into the vegetables.
5. Close the lid and flip the SmartSwitch to AIR FRY/HOB. Select SLOW COOK, set temperature to LOW, and set time to 9 hours. Press START/STOP to begin cooking, until the pork is soft.
6. Enjoy!

Traditional Jambalaya

SERVES: 6 TO 8

PREP TIME: 20 minutes
COOK TIME: 9½ hours

680 g raw prawns, shelled and deveined
10 (110-g) boneless, skinless chicken thighs, cut into 5 cm pieces
5 celery stalks, sliced
2 red chillies, minced
2 green bell peppers, stemmed, seeded, and chopped
500 ml chicken stock
2 onions, chopped
6 garlic cloves, minced
1 tbsp. Cajun seasoning
¼ tsp. cayenne pepper

1. Before getting started, be sure to remove the Cook & Crisp tray.
2. Mix the chicken, onions, garlic, red chillies, bell peppers, celery, chicken stock, Cajun seasoning, and cayenne in the bottom of the pot.
3. Close the lid and flip the SmartSwitch to AIR FRY/HOB. Select SLOW COOK, set temperature to LOW, and set time to 9 hours. Press START/STOP to begin cooking, until the chicken registers 74°C on a food thermometer.
4. Stir in the prawns. Close the lid and cook on low for an additional 30 to 40 minutes, or until the prawns are curled and pink. Serve warm.

Thai Beef Roast and Tomato

SERVES: 10

PREP TIME: 14 minutes
COOK TIME: 9 hours

1.1 kg grass-fed beef sirloin roast, cut into 5 cm pieces
3 large tomatoes, seeded and chopped
3 large carrots, shredded
3 onions, chopped
240 ml tinned coconut milk
180 ml peanut butter
6 garlic cloves, minced
125 ml beef stock
1 small red chili pepper, minced
2 tbsps. grated fresh ginger root
45 ml lime juice

1. Before getting started, be sure to remove the Cook & Crisp tray.
2. Mix the onions, garlic, carrots, ginger root, and tomatoes in the bottom of the pot.
3. In a medium bowl, mix the coconut milk, peanut butter, chili pepper, lime juice, and beef stock until blended well.
4. Place the roast on top of the vegetables in the pot and pour the peanut sauce over all.
5. Close the lid and flip the SmartSwitch to AIR FRY/HOB. Select SLOW COOK, set temperature to LOW, and set time to 9 hours. Press START/STOP to begin cooking, until the beef is very soft.
6. Serve warm.

Spicy Barbecue Chicken

SERVES: 4

PREP TIME: 6 minutes
COOK TIME: 7 hours

8 (170-g) boneless, skinless chicken breasts
2 (225-g) BPA-free tins no-salt-added tomato sauce
85 ml mustard
2 onions, minced
8 garlic cloves, minced
45 ml molasses
30 ml lemon juice
1 tbsp. chilli powder
2 tsps. paprika
¼ tsp. cayenne pepper

1. Before getting started, be sure to remove the Cook & Crisp tray.
2. Mix the tomato sauce, onions, garlic, mustard, lemon juice, molasses, chilli powder, paprika, and cayenne in the bottom of the pot.
3. Place the chicken and move the chicken around in the sauce with tongs to coat.
4. Close the lid and flip the SmartSwitch to AIR FRY/HOB. Select SLOW COOK, set temperature to LOW, and set time to 7 hours. Press START/STOP to begin cooking, until the chicken registers 74ºC on a food thermometer.
5. Serve warm.

Chicken with Squash and Mushroom

SERVES: 10

PREP TIME: 18 minutes
COOK TIME: 8 hours

1 (1.4-kg) butternut squash, peeled, seeded, and cut into 2.5 cm pieces
2 (450-g) acorn squash, peeled, seeded, and cut into 2.5 cm pieces
8 (170-g) bone-in, skinless chicken breasts
1 (225-g) package chestnut mushrooms, sliced
250 ml chicken stock
2 fennel bulbs, cored and sliced
3 sprigs fresh thyme
120 ml canned coconut milk
30 ml lemon juice
1 bay leaf

1. Before getting started, be sure to remove the Cook & Crisp tray.
2. Mix the butternut squash, acorn squash, fennel, mushrooms, chicken, chicken stock, thyme, bay leaf, and coconut milk in the bottom of the pot.
3. Close the lid and flip the SmartSwitch to AIR FRY/HOB. Select SLOW COOK, set temperature to LOW, and set time to 8 hours. Press START/STOP to begin cooking, until the chicken registers 74°C on a food thermometer.
4. Remove the thyme sprigs and bay leaf and discard. Stir in the lemon juice and serve warm.

Chickpea and Carrot Soup

SERVES: 7

PREP TIME: 20 minutes
COOK TIME: 6 hours

2 (425-g) BPA-free tins no-salt-added chickpeas, drained and rinsed
2 (400-g) BPA-free tins diced tomatoes, undrained
4 carrots, peeled and cut into chunks
2 medium parsley roots, peeled and sliced
2 onions, chopped
3 garlic cloves, minced
1.5 L vegetable broth
1 tsp. dried basil leaves
¼ tsp. freshly ground black pepper

1. Before getting started, be sure to remove the Cook & Crisp tray.
2. Layer all the ingredients in the bottom of the pot.
3. Close the lid and flip the SmartSwitch to AIR FRY/HOB. Select SLOW COOK, set temperature to LOW, and set time to 6 hours. Press START/STOP to begin cooking, until the vegetables are soft.
4. Stir in the soup and top with pesto, if desired. Serve warm.

Traditional Succotash with Tomato

SERVES: 10

PREP TIME: 14 minutes
COOK TIME: 8 hours

600g frozen corn
4 large tomatoes, seeded and chopped
350 g dry lima beans, rinsed and drained
1.2 L vegetable broth
1 red onion, minced
1 bay leaf
1 tsp. dried basil leaves
1 tsp. dried thyme leaves

1. Before getting started, be sure to remove the Cook & Crisp tray.
2. Mix all the ingredients in the bottom of the pot.
3. Close the lid and flip the SmartSwitch to AIR FRY/HOB. Select SLOW COOK, set temperature to LOW, and set time to 8 hours. Press START/STOP to begin cooking, until the lima beans are soft.
4. Remove the bay leaf and discard. Serve warm.

Mushroom Barley Risotto

SERVES: 6 TO 8

PREP TIME: 12 minutes
COOK TIME: 7 hours

1 (227 g) package button mushrooms, chopped
375 g hulled barley, rinsed
1.5 L low-sodium vegetable broth
150 g grated Parmesan cheese
1 onion, finely chopped
4 garlic cloves, minced
½ tsp. dried marjoram leaves
⅛ tsp. freshly ground black pepper

1. Before getting started, be sure to remove the Cook & Crisp tray.
2. Mix the barley, onion, garlic, mushrooms, broth, marjoram, and pepper in the bottom of the pot.
3. Close the lid and flip the SmartSwitch to AIR FRY/HOB. Select SLOW COOK, set temperature to LOW, and set time to 7 hours. Press START/STOP to begin cooking, until the barley has absorbed most of the liquid and is soft, and the vegetables are tender.
4. Toss in the Parmesan cheese and serve warm.

Garlic-Parmesan Pork and Potato

SERVES: 12

PREP TIME: 23 minutes
COOK TIME: 8 hours

1 (1.4-kg) boneless pork loin
900 g small creamer potatoes, rinsed
4 large carrots, cut into chunks
250 ml chicken stock
50 g grated Parmesan cheese
1 onion, chopped
12 garlic cloves, divided
1 tsp. dried marjoram leaves

1. Before getting started, be sure to remove the Cook & Crisp tray.
2. Mix the potatoes, carrots, and onions in the bottom of the pot.
3. Mince 6 of the garlic cloves and put them to the vegetables.
4. Slice the remaining 6 garlic cloves into slivers. Use a sharp knife to poke holes in the pork loin and place a garlic sliver into each hole.
5. Arrange the pork loin on the vegetables in the pot.
6. Pour the chicken stock over all and scatter with the marjoram.
7. Close the lid and flip the SmartSwitch to AIR FRY/HOB. Select SLOW COOK, set temperature to LOW, and set time to 8 hours. Press START/STOP to begin cooking, until the pork is tender.
8. Sprinkle with the Parmesan cheese and serve warm.

Vegan Pasta Stew

SERVES: 6

PREP TIME: 9 minutes
COOK TIME: 6½ hours

355 g whole-wheat orzo pasta
6 large tomatoes, seeded and chopped
2 L vegetable broth
340 g chopped yellow summer squash
225 g sliced button mushrooms
225 g sliced chestnut mushrooms
2 red bell peppers, stemmed, seeded, and chopped
2 onions, chopped
5 garlic cloves, minced
2 tsps. dried Italian seasoning

1. Before getting started, be sure to remove the Cook & Crisp tray.
2. Mix the onions, garlic, mushrooms, bell peppers, summer squash, tomatoes, vegetable broth, and Italian seasoning in the bottom of the pot.
3. Close the lid and flip the SmartSwitch to AIR FRY/HOB. Select SLOW COOK, set temperature to LOW, and set time to 6 hours. Press START/STOP to begin cooking, until the vegetables are soft.
4. When the time is up, open the lid and place the pasta to the pot, stirring. Close the lid and cook on low for 20 to 30 minutes, until the pasta is tender.
5. Serve warm.

Colourful Carrot with Poached Trout

SERVES: 8

PREP TIME: 15 minutes
COOK TIME: 8½ hours

6 (140 g each) trout fillets
4 large orange carrots, peeled and sliced
3 purple carrots, peeled and sliced
3 yellow carrots, peeled and sliced
120 ml vegetable broth or fish stock
2 onions, chopped
4 garlic cloves, minced
1 bay leaf
1 tsp. dried marjoram leaves
½ tsp. salt

1. Before getting started, be sure to remove the Cook & Crisp tray.
2. Mix the carrots, onions, garlic, vegetable broth, marjoram, bay leaf, and salt in the bottom of the pot.
3. Close the lid and flip the SmartSwitch to AIR FRY/HOB. Select SLOW COOK, set temperature to LOW, and set time to 8 hours. Press START/STOP to begin cooking, until the carrots are soft.
4. When the time is up, open the lid. Remove the bay leaf and discard. Place the trout fillets to the pot. Close the lid and cook on low for another 20 to 30 minutes, or until the fish flakes when tested with a fork.
5. Enjoy!

French Chicken, Mushroom and Wild Rice Stew

SERVES: 9

PREP TIME: 14 minutes
COOK TIME: 8 hours

10 boneless, skinless chicken thighs, cut into 5 cm pieces
2 (400-g) BPA-free tins diced tomatoes, undrained
3 large carrots, sliced
2 leeks, chopped
2 L vegetable broth
150 g sliced chestnut mushrooms
185 g wild rice, rinsed and drained
60 g sliced ripe olives
3 garlic cloves, minced
2 tsp. dried herbes de Provence

1. Before getting started, be sure to remove the Cook & Crisp tray.
2. Mix all the ingredients in the bottom of the pot.
3. Close the lid and flip the SmartSwitch to AIR FRY/HOB. Select SLOW COOK, set temperature to LOW, and set time to 8 hours. Press START/STOP to begin cooking, until the chicken is cooked to 74°C and the wild rice is soft.
4. Serve warm.

Prawn and Polenta with Tomato

SERVES: 9

PREP TIME: 16 minutes
COOK TIME: 6½ hours

900 g raw prawns, peeled and deveined
4 large tomatoes, seeded and chopped
440 g polenta
2 L chicken stock or vegetable broth
2 onions, chopped
2 green bell peppers, stemmed, seeded, and chopped
170 g shredded Cheddar cheese
5 garlic cloves, minced
1 bay leaf
1 tsp. Old Bay Seasoning

1. Before getting started, be sure to remove the Cook & Crisp tray.
2. Mix the polenta, onions, garlic, tomatoes, bell peppers, chicken stock, bay leaf, and seasoning in the bottom of the pot.
3. Close the lid and flip the SmartSwitch to AIR FRY/HOB. Select SLOW COOK, set temperature to LOW, and set time to 6 hours. Press START/STOP to begin cooking, until the polenta are soft and most of the liquid is absorbed.
4. When the time is up, open the lid and place the prawns, stirring. Close the lid and cook on low for 30 to 40 minutes, until the prawns are curled and pink.
5. Stir in the cheese and serve warm.

French Asparagus and Courgette Omelette

SERVES: 6

PREP TIME: 16 minutes
COOK TIME: 4 hours

12 eggs, beaten
225 g chopped fresh asparagus
1 small courgette, peeled and diced
1 yellow bell pepper, stemmed, seeded, and chopped
50 g grated Parmesan cheese
80 ml semi-skimmed milk
2 shallots, peeled and minced
½ tsp. dried tarragon leaves
½ tsp. dried thyme leaves
¼ tsp. salt

1. Before getting started, be sure to remove the Cook & Crisp tray.
2. Mix the eggs, milk, thyme, tarragon, and salt in a large bowl, and mix well with an eggbeater or wire whisk until well combined.
3. Place the asparagus, courgette, bell pepper, and shallots into the the bottom of the pot.
4. Close the lid and flip the SmartSwitch to AIR FRY/HOB. Select SLOW COOK, set temperature to "Buffet", and set time to 4 hours. Press START/STOP to begin cooking, until the eggs are set.
5. With 10 minutes remaining, open the lid. Scatter with the Parmesan cheese. Close the lid to continue cooking, until the cheese starts to melt.
6. Enjoy!

Honey Carrot Oat Cake

SERVES: 6

PREP TIME: 12 minutes
COOK TIME: 7 hours

30 ml melted coconut oil
360 g coarse oatmeal
225 g BPA-free tin of unsweetened crushed pineapple in juice, undrained
1 L water
500 ml almond milk
240 g finely grated carrot
60 ml honey
2 tsps. vanilla extract
1 tsp. ground cinnamon
¼ tsp. salt

1. Before getting started, be sure to remove the Cook & Crisp tray.
2. Grease the bottom of the pot with coconut oil.
3. Mix the coarse oatmeal, carrot, and pineapple in the bottom of the pot.
4. Mix the almond milk, water, coconut oil, honey, vanilla, salt, and cinnamon in a medium bowl. Mix until combined well. Add this mixture into the pot.
5. Close the lid and flip the SmartSwitch to AIR FRY/HOB. Select SLOW COOK, set temperature to LOW, and set time to 7 hours. Press START/STOP to begin cooking, until the oatmeal is tender and the edges start to brown.
6. Enjoy!

APPENDIX 1: 4-WEEK MEAL PLAN

Week-1	Breakfast	Lunch	Dinner	Snack/Dessert
Day-1	• Banana and Walnut Cake	• Cheesy Chicken Stuffed Mushrooms	• Ranch Dipped Fillets	• Frosting Cupcakes
Day-2	• Cheesy Potato Patties	• Bacon Wrapped Filet Mignon with Bean Rice	• Chickpea and Carrot Soup	• Tortilla Chips
Day-3	• Homemade Chicken Fajitas	• Chicken Manchurian	• Lush Vegetables Roast	• Cajun Courgette Crisps
Day-4	• Courgette and Mushroom Pizza	• Thai Coconut Curry Lamb	• Five Spice Pork and Quinoa with Asparagus	• Rich Layered Cake
Day-5	• Beef and Kale Omelette	• Scallops with Spinach and Quinoa	• Simple Ribeye Steak	• Old-Fashioned Onion Rings
Day-6	• Vanilla Blueberry Cake	• French Chicken, Mushroom and Wild Rice Stew	• Pork Neck and Tomato Salad	• Crispy Apple Crisps
Day-7	• Trout Frittata	• Asian Chicken with Courgette Pasta	• Mushroom Barley Risotto	• Crunchy Chickpeas

Week-2	Breakfast	Lunch	Dinner	Snack/Dessert
Day-1	• French Asparagus and Courgette Omelette	• Coated Prawn and Cherry Tomato Meal	• Chicken with Squash and Mushroom	• Tropical Fruit Sticks
Day-2	• Doughnuts Pudding	• Turkey Breast with Herb	• Bacon Filled Poppers	• Super Moist Chocolate Cake
Day-3	• Healthy Egg Veggie Frittata	• Traditional Succotash with Tomato	• Miso Marinated Steak and Spinach Pasta	• Honey-Roasted Pears with Walnuts
Day-4	• Nutmeg Pumpkin Pudding	• Rosemary Duck Breasts	• Pork and Carrot with Scallion	• Rich Layered Cake
Day-5	• Panko Salmon Patties	• Salmon and Bok Choy Meal	• Colourful Carrot with Poached Trout	• Herbed Pitta Crisps
Day-6	• Beef Cheeseburgers	• Glazed Pork and Broccoli Rice	• Balsamic Bok Choy	• Honey Carrot Oat Cake
Day-7	• Fudgy Chocolaty Squares	• Broccoli and Chicken	• BBQ Pork Steaks	• Crispy Breaded Olives

Week-3	Breakfast	Lunch	Dinner	Snack/Dessert
Day-1	• Courgette and Mushroom Pizza	• Pork and Brussels Sprouts with Oyster Sauce	• Chicken with Butternut Squash Porridge	• Butter Apple Roll-Ups
Day-2	• Nutmeg Pumpkin Pudding	• Mustard Lamb Ribs	• Vegan Pasta Stew	• Tropical Fruit Sticks
Day-3	• Beef and Kale Omelette	• Beef Bratwursts with Quinoa	• Honey Cod with Sesame Seeds	• Frosting Cupcakes
Day-4	• Doughnuts Pudding	• Sweet Beef and Mango Skewers	• Homemade Pulled Pork	• Crispy Apple Crisps
Day-5	• Cheesy Potato Patties	• Barbecue Chicken	• Pesto Coated Rack of Lamb and Farfalle	• Tortilla Chips
Day-6	• Fudgy Chocolaty Squares	• Citrus Roasted Pork	• Lemon Pork Tenderloin	• Crispy Breaded Olives
Day-7	• Banana and Walnut Cake	• Turmeric Chicken Thighs	• Mongolian Beef	• Honey-Roasted Pears with Walnuts

Week-4	Breakfast	Lunch	Dinner	Snack/Dessert
Day-1	• Panko Salmon Patties	• Beef and Sugar Snap with Sha Cha	• Garlic-Lemon Tilapia with Mushroom Rice	• Old-Fashioned Onion Rings
Day-2	• Beef Cheeseburgers	• Pine Nut Pork and Olive Pasta	• Whangarei Style Mussels	• Cajun Courgette Crisps
Day-3	• Trout Frittata	• Garlic Soy Chicken Thighs	• Traditional Jambalaya	• Honey Carrot Oat Cake
Day-4	• Vanilla Blueberry Cake	• Thai Beef Roast and Tomato	• Coconut Crusted Prawn	• Crunchy Chickpeas
Day-5	• French Asparagus and Courgette Omelette	• Classic Kerala Curry	• Spiced Lamb Steaks and Snap Pea Rice	• Super Moist Chocolate Cake
Day-6	• Homemade Chicken Fajitas	• Chicken and Pepper Meatballs	• Drunken Prawns	• Butter Apple Roll-Ups
Day-7	• Healthy Egg Veggie Frittata	• Paprika Chicken Drumsticks with Chickpea Rice	• Honey Cod with Sesame Seeds	• Herbed Pitta Crisps

APPENDIX 2: NINJA SPEEDI TIMETABLE

Steam Air Fry Chart

INGREDIENT	AMOUNT	PREPARATION	WATER	ORIENTATION	TEMP	COOK TIME
POULTRY						
Chicken breasts	2 (175g each)	None	125ml	Top	190°C	15-20 mins
Chicken breasts, breaded	4 (175g each)	None	125ml	Top	190°C	18-20 mins
Chicken drumsticks	1kg	None	125ml	Top	210°C	25-30 mins
Chicken thighs (bone in)	1kg	None	125ml	Top	190°C	20-25 mins
Chicken thighs (boneless)	4 (100-125g each)	None	125ml	Top	190°C	15-18 mins
Chicken wings	500g	None	125ml	Bottom	220°C	15 mins
Whole chicken	2-2.5kg	Trussed	250ml	Bottom	180°C	60-80 mins
Turkey breast	1.4-2.4kg	None	250ml	Bottom	180°C	45-55 mins
BEEF						
Topside	1.5kg	None	250ml	Bottom	180°C	45 mins for medium rare
Rolled rib	1.5kg	None	250ml	Bottom	180°C	30-32 mins for medium rare
PORK						
Pork chops	4 thick-cut, bone-in (250g each)	Bone in	125ml	Top	190°C	25-30 mins
Pork chops	4 boneless (100-125g each)	Boneless	125ml	Top	190°C	20-25 mins
Pork loin	1kg	None	250ml	Bottom	180°C	35-40 mins
LAMB						
Leg of lamb	1.5kg	None	250ml	Bottom	180°C	37-40 mins
FISH						
Cod	4 (150g each)	None	125ml	Top	220°C	9-12 mins
Salmon	4 (150g each)	None	65ml	Top	220°C	7-10 mins

*NOTE: Crisper tray position varies, as specified in chart. Steam will take approximately 4-10 minutes to build.

Steam Air Fry Chart

INGREDIENT	AMOUNT	PREPARATION	WATER	ORIENTATION	TEMP	COOK TIME
FROZEN POULTRY						
Chicken breasts	4 (175g each)	None	250ml	Top	200°C	15-20 mins
Chicken drumsticks	1kg	None	125ml	Top	180°C	20-25 mins
Chicken thighs	1kg	None	125ml	Top	200°C	20-22 mins
Chicken wings	500g	None	125ml	Bottom	220°C	15 mins
FROZEN BEEF						
Steak, sirloin	2 (225g each)	None	250ml	Top	180°C	12-18 mins
FROZEN FISH						
Salmon	4 (120g each)	None	65ml	Top	220°C	7-10 mins
Cod	4 (120g each)	None	125ml	Top	220°C	10-15 mins
FROZEN PORK						
Pork chops with bone	2 (250g each)	None	125ml	Bottom	190°C	23-28 mins
Sausages	450g	None	125ml	Bottom	190°C	10-12 mins
VEGETABLES						
Beetroot	1kg	Peel, cut into 1.25cm cubes	125ml	Bottom	200°C	30-35 mins
Broccoli	400g	Whole, remove stem	125ml	Bottom	210°C	15-20 mins
Brussels sprouts	1kg	Cut in half, trim ends	125ml	Bottom	220°C	10-12 mins
Butternut squash	1kg	Cut in half, deseed	125ml	Bottom	190°C	22-25 mins
Carrots	1kg	Peel, cut into 1.25cm rounds	125ml	Bottom	200°C	22-28 mins
Parsnip	500g	Cut into 2.5cm pieces	125ml	Bottom	200°C	30-35 mins
Potatoes, King Edward/Maris Piper/Russet	1kg	Cut into 2.5cm wedges	125ml	Bottom	220°C	30-35 mins
	4, 800g	Whole	125ml	Bottom	200°C	25-30 mins
Sweet potatoes	1kg	Cut into 2.5cm cubes	125ml	Bottom	200°C	20 mins

*NOTE: Crisper tray position varies, as specified in chart. Steam will take approximately 4-10 minutes to build.

Air Fry Chart for the Crisper Tray, bottom position

INGREDIENT	AMOUNT	PREPARATION	OIL	TEMP	COOK TIME
VEGETABLES					
Asparagus	250g	Trim stems	2 tsp	200°C	7-8 mins
Bell peppers	4 (750g)	Whole	None	200°C	20 mins
Cauliflower	400g	Cut in 2.5-5cm florets	1 tbsp	200°C	12-14 mins
Corn on the cob	4 ears (1kg)	Whole ears, husk removed	1 tbsp	200°C	12-15 mins
Courgette	500g	Cut in quarters lengthwise, then into 2.5cm pieces	1 tbsp	200°C	11-12 mins
Green beans	350g	Trimmed	1 tbsp	200°C	7-10 mins
Kale for chips	400g	Torn in pieces, stems removed	None	150°C	8-12 mins
Mushrooms	300g	Wipe, quarter	1 tbsp	200°C	7-8 mins
Potatoes, King Edward/Maris Piper/Russets	500g	Hand cut chips, thin	½-3 tbsp	200°C	18-22 mins
	500g	Hand cut chips, thick	½-3 tbsp	200°C	20-22 mins
Potatoes, sweet	1kg	Cut into 2.5cm cubes	1 tbsp	200°C	14-16 mins
BEEF					
Burgers	4 (125g each)	1.5-1.75cm thick	None	190°C	10 mins
Steak	2 (225g each)	None	Brushed with oil	200°C	8-12 mins
PORK					
Bacon	6 rashers, (200g)	Lay rashers evenly over tray	None	170°C	10 mins
Gammon steak	1 (225g)	Whole	None	200°C	10-12 mins
Sausages	8 (450g)	None	None	200°C	7-8 mins

*TIP When using Air Fry, add 5 minutes to the suggested cook time for the unit to preheat before you add ingredients.

Air Fry Chart for the Crisper Tray, bottom position

INGREDIENT	AMOUNT	PREPARATION	OIL	TEMP	COOK TIME
FROZEN FOODS					
Chicken nuggets	380g	None	None	200°C	10 mins
Fish fillets (battered)	440g	None	None	200°C	14 mins
Fish fingers	10 (280g)	None	None	200°C	9-10 mins
Hash browns	8 (360g)	None	None	200°C	14 mins
Roast potatoes	700g	None	None	200°C	25-30 mins
Mozzarella sticks	360g	None	None	200°C	6-7 mins
Onion rings	300g	None	None	200°C	10-12 mins
Scampi	9 jumbo pieces (230g)	None	None	200°C	7 mins
Sweet potato fries	500g	None	None	200°C	15 mins
Veggie burgers	4 (350g)	None	None	190°C	14 mins
Veggie sausages	6 (270g)	None	None	200°C	7-8 mins
FROZEN CHIPS					
Light straight chips	500g	None	None	200°C	14 mins
Chunky chips	500g	None	None	200°C	17 mins
Crinkle cut chips	500g	None	None	200°C	16 mins
French fries	500g	None	None	180°C	14 mins
Gastro chips	700g	None	None	200°C	18-20 mins
Potato wedges	650g	None	None	200°C	15 mins
Skin-on chips	500g	None	None	200°C	16-17 mins
FISH & SEAFOOD					
Fishcakes	2 (150g each)	None	None	200°C	8-10 mins
Prawns	16 jumbo	Raw, whole, tails on	1 tbsp	200°C	7-10 mins

*TIP When using Air Fry, add 5 minutes to the suggested cook time for the unit to preheat before you add ingredients.

Steam Chart for the Crisper Tray, bottom position

INGREDIENT	AMOUNT	PREPARATION	LIQUID	COOK TIME
VEGETABLES				
Asparagus	250g	Whole spears	250ml	5-7 mins
Broccoli	300g	Cut into 2.5-5cm florets	250ml	5-9 mins
Brussels sprouts	400g	Whole, trimmed	250ml	10-15 mins
Butternut squash	500g	Peeled, cut into 2.5cm cubes	250ml	10-15 mins
Carrots	500g	Peeled, cut into 2.5cm pieces	250ml	10-15 mins
Cauliflower	400g	Peeled, cut into 2.5-5cm florets	250ml	5-10 mins
Corn on the cob	4 ears	Whole, husks removed	250ml	8-10 mins
Green beans	200g	Whole, trimmed	250ml	8-12 mins
Potatoes	500g	Peeled, cut into 2.5cm pieces	325ml	12-17 mins
Potatoes, baby new	500g	Whole pieces	325ml	15-20 mins
Sweet potatoes	500g	Cut into 1.25cm cubes	250ml	8-14 mins

Dehydrate Chart for the Crisper Tray, bottom position

INGREDIENT	PREPARATION	TEMP	DEHYDRATE TIME
FRUITS & VEGETABLES			
Apple chips	Cut into 3mm slices, remove core, rinse in lemon water, pat dry	60°C	7-8 hrs
Bananas	Peel, cut into 3mm slices	60°C	8-10 hrs
Fresh herbs	Rinse, pat dry, remove stems	60°C	4-6 hrs
Ginger root	Cut into 3mm slices	60°C	6 hrs
Mangoes	Peel, cut into 3mm slices, remove stone	60°C	6-8 hrs
Mushrooms	Clean with soft brush or wipe with damp kitchen paper	60°C	6-8 hrs
Pineapple	Peel, cut into 3mm-1.25cm slices, core removed	60°C	6-8 hrs
Strawberries	Cut in half or into 1.25cm slices	60°C	6-8 hrs
Tomatoes	Cut into 3mm slices; steam if planning to rehydrate	60°C	6-8 hrs
MEAT, POULTRY, FISH			
Beef, chicken, salmon jerky	Cut into 6mm slices, marinate overnight	70°C	5-7 hrs

*TIP Most fruits and vegetables take between 6 and 8 hours (at 60°C) to dehydrate; meats take between 5 and 7 hours (at 70°C). The longer you dehydrate your ingredients, the crispier they will be.

APPENDIX 3: RECIPES INDEX

Printed in Great Britain
by Amazon

25859691R00046